REAL SERVICE

Raven Kaldera and Joshua Tenpenny

REAL
SERVICE

Raven Kaldera
and Joshua Tenpenny

Alfred Press
Hubbardston, Massachusetts

Alfred Press
12 Simond Hill Road
Hubbardston, MA 01452

Real Service
© 2011 Raven Kaldera and Joshua Tenpenny
ISBN   978-0-9828794-3-6

Printed in cooperation with
Lulu Enterprises, Inc.
860 Aviation Parkway, Suite 300
Morrisville, NC 27560

Dedicated to all the new M/s folks out there who believe that yes, this life can really work. We were where you are once. We assure you that you're right.

Contents

Introduction: Basic Assumptions

When we began to assemble this book, we assumed that our readership would be entirely composed of *service-oriented submissives*. By that, we mean individuals who have (or want to have) a relationship where they put a substantial portion of their time and energy towards rendering personal service of some kind to someone else, under that person's direction and guidance, and with the desire to conform to their will. (If you are a servant of some sort and don't identify with this label, we apologize.) As we wrote, however, we realized that this information was also relevant to people who are not particularly submissive or not particularly fond of service, but are nevertheless involved in service-based relationships where they serve or are under the authority of another person. We don't specifically address the unique challenges faced by people in those situations, but we do hope that what we write will be of some use to them.

In addition, we also realized that people on the receiving-service and giving-orders end needed to learn about service as well, and we began to write sections that were specifically geared toward dominants, masters, mistresses, and the rest of the People In Charge. There are many M-types out there who would like to receive better service, but they're not sure how to manage things in order to get it. They may also not be quite sure what it looks like, depending on the social group they grew up in. That's why there are some sections addressed directly to them.

We are not addressing the issues involved in rendering service to people over whom one has no authority or control, or service rendered reciprocally. The type of service covered in this book is a decidedly inegalitarian type of service which defers to the will of another person, at least with regard to the manner in which service is provided. As such, any statements about what service is or isn't should be understood in that context, and may not apply to more dominant styles of service.

The other labels we will use are "servant" and "master" to refer to individuals actively engaged in a service relationship, and "s-type" and "M-type" as umbrella terms for people who are involved in some kind of a power dynamic. That's our term for a negotiated inegalitarian relationship – power dynamic. We use the term "relationship" without intending to imply romantic or intimate connection. We do not assume for any particular gender combination, and unless clearly specified, gendered references throughout the book are arbitrary. Unless we are specifically addressing issues of relationships involving three or more people, for simplicity we will generally refer to relationships between one master and one servant.

The style of service we describe may seem excessively deferential or submissive to suit some servants, and we generally imply the servant should be entirely willing to do everything exactly as the master wants. Obviously, different service relationships have different boundaries. We make no assumptions, unless otherwise specified, about the degree of authority or control a master ought to have over the servant's life. We are well aware that power dynamics come in a wide range of control and limits and intensity, and we hope that our observations about service will hold true for all the points on that continuum. The servant is only assumed to sincerely desire to conform to the will of the master with regard to the topic under discussion, if that topic is relevant to their service and within the scope of their service relationship.

While we hope that, in theory, this information might be useful to a wide range of individuals interested in service-based relationships, our focus is really on people who approach this subject from the perspective of some type of BDSM or M/s (Master/slave) subculture, which we will refer to collectively and generically as "the scene". We have neither the time nor inclination to cover the basics of involvement in these activities, or the many differences between these subcultures, or between the peripheral subcultures also engaging in power dynamics, and that's really beside the point. We invite the reader to explore the many non-fiction introductory books available on BDSM and related topics if our examples of relationships, roles, or activities are confusing (or intriguing).

We are also aware that not all people who call themselves submissives or slaves are necessarily service-oriented, or interested in service at all (and, in addition, not all those who call themselves dominants, masters, and mistresses are necessarily interested in having skilled servants). On the contrary – our informal polling seems to have shown that more individuals on both sides of the slash are drawn to these lifestyles because of their attraction to control rather than service. Controlling others, or feeling the control of others, seems to be more popular as a motivation than service. However, even control-oriented masters require their slaves to do practical work sometimes, including tasks that they are interested in having done correctly and would prefer not to see screwed up, even if it's fun to "punish" someone.

The idea for this book came after we attended a workshop labeled "Service" at a BDSM conference which turned out to be almost entirely about caring for an M-type's leathers and boots, a bit about cigars, and little else. We were incredulous, but after some time we ceased to be surprised. There is a huge gulf between people who actually want to be useful and people who want to play at serving someone while only focusing on activities designed to arouse them. Around the same time, we were counseling a married couple that was new to M/s. The s-type was concerned that her husband wasn't interested in her serving him anymore, and she wanted to know what she could do make her service more appealing to him. It turned out that she was performing a range of "services" that she'd selected from fantasy depictions of M/s, and while he'd been humoring her for a while, they weren't especially appealing to him. For example, she had a special "service" routine worked out that she wanted to perform for him when he got home from work, but most nights, he was just too tired. When we asked the M-type what he'd ideally like from her when he came home from work, he sheepishly said, "Well, I'd like her to bring me a sandwich and a beer, and leave me alone for an hour." She'd only ever offered him heavily fetishy "service" activities, and despite her assurance she'd do "anything" for him, it never occurred to him that he could ask for simple real-world tasks.

We're a master/slave couple who both focus heavily on service – giving and receiving – and for whom it must be useful in a real way, in real life. Joshua might offer sexual service and clean Raven's boots, but he also drives Raven to doctor's appointments, maintains Raven's websites, does the taxes, makes homemade mayonnaise, scrubs out the bathtub, shops for groceries, runs errands, formats manuscripts, feeds the goats and sheep on our farm, and does a hundred other services both large and small that allow Raven to run his life in a more efficient way.

It's taken a decade to get the quality of his service to this point, and we still strive to improve it. Our description may not sound all that sexy, but it is hugely fulfilling for both of us. Raven gets another pair of hands to do almost anything he might want help with, and Joshua gets to feel competent and useful. He also knows that his work is making a difference beyond that of fetish activities. Both he and his master are proud of his service, and his favorite compliment from his master is to be called "My Resourceful Boy!"

This book was written for M-types who would like to develop a multi-skilled tool to help them live more effectively, and s-types who love to serve and know that there's so much more they could do, or at least would like to learn better service to please their M-type, regardless of whether it's their thing. It's not as hard as you think it might be … and parts of it are more complex than you know. Welcome to the world of Real Service, among the folks that Get Shit Done.

Figuring Out Service

Service Porn and the Butler Fetish

Perhaps in your fantasies, you fancy yourself as an English butler serving a wealthy master in a large manor on some remote scenic hillside. Or maybe you're a French maid in one of those fussy little dresses, serving high tea. Maybe you are a courtesan or a geisha. However, the chances are high that this will forever remain a fantasy role, not your real life. Fantasy is wonderful. Fantasy lets us express deep parts of ourselves that aren't nurtured by our day-to-day lives, and sometimes we can be more "real" in our fantasy than we can in normal society. We highly encourage people to explore and enact their fantasies in whatever ways they find mutually agreeable ... so long as they keep in mind that it isn't real life.

Some people have so much enthusiasm for these fantasies, or find in them such a deep expression of their core self, that they choose to make space in their lives for their favored roles on a day-to-day basis. When people in the scene say that "24/7" M/s relationships aren't possible, or aren't practical, or never work out in the real world, they are thinking about doing this kind of role-play all the time. We won't say that you can't live your entire life in a narrowly defined role, because some people actually do, in the scene and outside of it. We will say that it is a lot of work, and often breaks down when circumstances cause the demands of the "real world" to increase.

A service relationship can be role-based, but it doesn't have to be, and more often than not, it isn't. It can just be two (or more) people who have an arrangement where one has dedicated a substantial portion of their time and energy to the service of the other. There doesn't need to be any protocol, collars, or kinky sex. There doesn't need to be anything formal about it.

And we cannot say this emphatically enough: *there does not need to be anything "high-class" about it.* It doesn't need to involve any activities beyond what normal people in your usual social circle engage in. Too many service-oriented submissive become fixated on a perceived high-class role, and think that the way to prepare themselves for a service position is to learn what sort of wine goes with what, how to store and prepare cigars, how to serve a formal dinner, and perhaps how to dock a yacht. Personally, we don't know anyone with a yacht, and if you don't either, then your chances of ending up in service to someone who needs you to dock one are pretty slim. If formal dinners, tea service, and yachts really are part of your normal everyday world, then go ahead and throw yourself into that style of service. If not, it is best that you come to terms with this being a *fantasy role*. Accept that you have a butler fetish, and enjoy it for what it is.

This book, however, is not about fantasy roles. It is about regular people offering normal, everyday services to other regular people. If that isn't what you are looking for, no problem. This book isn't for you. But if you are looking for ways to incorporate real service into your everyday life, I hope this book gives you ideas about the wide variety of ways that any sincerely interested person can be of service to another person.

Joshua's Rules Of Service

The First Rule of Service is:
If the master doesn't want it, it isn't service.

I'll say that again: *If the master doesn't want it, it isn't service.*

Even if you are doing it for their benefit. Even if you think they ought to want it. Even if you think it needs to be done. Even if bad things will happen if it isn't done. Even if you are really good at it. Even if your last master loved it. Even if your mother taught you it is the way things are done. Even if doing it is traditionally associated with your role. Even if people in the scene expect you to do it. Even if you find it deeply fulfilling.

It isn't service. That doesn't mean no one should ever do it, or that it is wrong to want to do it. It just isn't service.

We've seen discussions about this on various online forums and in real-life groups, and often a harried M-type will admit to accepting service that they didn't want (or that they found unsatisfactory) in order to make the servant feel better. The more experienced servants have generally been horrified by the idea. They have pointed out that humoring a servant, and not letting them know that you don't want or like the service they're giving, is unacceptable in many ways, including:

- It's dishonest – the master is basically lying to them.
- It assumes that they are too emotionally fragile to handle any correction.
- It assumes that they are not competent enough to be worth training to do a good job.
- It does not give them accurate feedback on their service, and thus they cannot improve – and a good servant wants to constantly improve themselves and their service.
- It means that they've wasted their time on something unappreciated.
- It means that the master isn't really the one in charge. The servant's emotional reactions, or the master's fears about the servant's emotional reactions, are what's really in charge.

While acquiescence may seem like a favor to the bright-eyed well-meaning servant, in the end it is no favor. Honesty is the best option. Many masters find that having very high and exacting standards brings out the best in their servants, and I don't know any service-oriented submissives who dream of finding a master who has low expectations. But while the majority of s-types interested in service relationships have the emotional maturity and self-confidence to handle constructive criticism, many others have long-established patterns of emotional neediness in order to fulfill their desire for service or submission. Also, many think that being emotionally devastated by the slightest criticism shows the sincerity of their submission, and that to accept criticism without distress would be inappropriate for their role. It may take a firm and skilled master to break through this type of servant's established role to reveal their genuine strength and emotional resilience. They may benefit from a formal training program where they begin in a very restricted role with no duties and extremely limited free expression, and gradually earn the right to render service to their master and express themselves more freely.

On the other hand, some s-types really do need a more emotionally supportive situation, and would be devastated by firm handling and strict rules. With a truly emotionally vulnerable servant, a master might praise them enthusiastically for their *effort*, and then offer them guidance in how they can more appropriately direct that effort into effective service, or praise them for how much progress they've made while still making it clear that there is room for improvement. However, once a behavior pattern like this is established, breaking out of it generally involves a significant shift in the basis of the relationship. For example, in a "Daddy/boy" type relationship it is not uncommon for the "Daddy" to be extremely emotionally nurturing in the early stages of the relationship, and over time the "boy" is helped to "grow up" into a more adult role where they don't require such extensive caretaking.

The Second Rule of Service is: Contempt has no place in service.

If either person feels contempt for the other, something has gone very wrong. A service relationship should ideally be one of mutual respect – the servant respects the master or they wouldn't be serving them, and the master respects the servant's calling as a worthy and honorable one. Contempt in either direction will become apparent in even the most careful and formal of dynamics, and it won't take long for both parties to slowly begin to dislike each other and their interactions.

Even in extreme cases where the master and servant are both comfortable with the idea that the master is in some way inherently superior to the servant, if the master has contempt for the servant or their role, it shows that the master is not secure in their "superior" role. They should fully understand both their own right to give orders, and that following orders is not an act of degradation. When this is understood, service can be managed and received with graciousness, not disdain or condescension.

In most cases where contempt is flowing from the top down, it's usually not so much about the servant personally as it is contempt for service roles in general. We're taught – at least in many parts of modern Western society – that service jobs are degrading, something to be avoided unless you clearly can't do anything better, to be abandoned as soon as you get a "better" job. From this point of view, someone who actively seeks a service role must have something wrong with them as a person; perhaps they are so pathetic that they can't do any better. At the same time, many masters who have unfortunately absorbed this way of thinking do want to be served, so they are faced with an internal conflict between the joy of receiving good service and the discomfort of depending on someone who is, by their measure, worthy only of contempt for their choices. It's the reason why many people treat waitstaff badly or verbally abuse cashiers, and it has no place in a healthy service relationship. A good servant is both a valuable resource and a skilled worker doing what they enjoy.

There's an excellent vignette about this problem in the first season of the British miniseries *Downton Abbey*, where a middle-class solicitor (lawyer) is made the heir of a rich and aristocratic family, and assigned a valet. He is uncomfortable with being served in this very personal way, and his contempt for the valet and servants in general shows through with comments like, "It seems like a foolish job for a grown man to be doing." Eventually the lord of the manor takes him to task, pointing out that the valet enjoys his job and is good at it, and part of their job as employers is to give him a place to do his work. This opens the solicitor's eyes enough so that he is able to accept personal service more gracefully and with more respect.

Perhaps more difficult to recognize is servants who feel some level of contempt for their masters. In a society uncomfortable with service, it is common for people in a socially-devalued service position to find a sense of pride in feeling somehow superior to the people they serve. You see this in secretaries who enjoy the fact that their boss can't find anything in the office alone, and in bitter wives who treat their husbands like overgrown children who need to be kept out of the kitchen. A perfect example is, ironically, one of the most iconic fictional representations of service. Jeeves, from the series of novels by P.G. Wodehouse, is portrayed as in every way superior to his master Bertie Wooster, and while Jeeves is clearly devoted to Wooster, he generally treats Wooster like an idiot child under his care. Jeeves routinely goes against his master's wishes and manipulates him into whatever course of behavior Jeeves has decided upon, and occasionally destroys his master's possessions if he deems them to be in poor taste.

There is nothing wrong with the servant honestly believing that the master would find it difficult or impossible to do certain things without the servant's assistance, provided there is no contempt for the master in this assessment. However, if the servant desperately wants to be indispensible to the master, it can lead to inappropriate behaviors, such as setting things up in an intentionally obscure way or making it needlessly difficult for anyone else to perform the servant's tasks. Such a servant is generally very jealous of anyone else offering service to their master, and extremely resistant to delegating or accepting assistance from any other servants. While the relationship would certainly benefit from the servant resolving whatever deep emotional issue is involved here, this sort of attitude doesn't necessarily destroy a relationship. On the other hand, if the servant consistently feels better about themselves when they think about the master's shortcomings, or finds themselves hoping the master will fail, this attitude will certainly poison the relationship unless it is completely eradicated.

The Third Rule of Service is:
A bad attitude is corrosive to the servant and the relationship.

We've probably all had to deal with the issue of paid service personnel who go about their jobs with a sullen or hostile attitude, clearly hating what they're doing. While many of them may be forced by economic circumstances into doing service work that they are not suited for, consensual servants don't have that excuse. That doesn't always stop them from having a lousy attitude, of course. Servants sometimes use sulking or bitching while they work as a stress outlet and feel somewhat better afterwards, but we believe that it's more of a problem in the long run than they might believe.

Some masters don't care if their servant goes about grumbling, so long as the job gets done and they don't have to hear it. Some don't even care about hearing it, so long as there is no actual disobedience. While the master may not mind, the person who is most harmed by serving with a bad attitude is the servant. Eventually, over time, service will become associated in subtle ways with unpleasantness, and they will begin to hate their job, and perhaps the master who is the hub of that job. To keep going day after day in a service relationship, the servant must make an ongoing effort to associate service with happiness and contentment as often as possible, and this means actively working to find ways to have a good attitude.

One way to find a better attitude is to strive for excellence in service, even when it doesn't seem like an "important" task. For many servants, the majority of their work is not important tasks, but simple, repetitive, low-priority tasks. Many s-types find it more fulfilling to do a task according to very specific instructions or to a very high standard rather than just grinding through and getting it done. Tackling a precision job with all their energy and getting the master's well-earned approval can be very satisfying for them. Masters should consider the idea that if the servant doesn't like a particular task, making it more of a challenge might actually get them to like it more. (And if it turns out that you make it harder and they hate it even more, when you go back to the original way it will seem so much easier in comparison.)

The Fourth Rule of Service is:
   A good servant wants their master to be right.

The rule isn't "A good servant *wishes* their master *was* always right." Masters are human, and sometimes they are wrong. However, when the master and the servant disagree about what is the right way to do something, a good servant wants their master's decision to work out well, even if that means the servant was wrong. Servants are human too, and sometimes they are wrong. Most people have no trouble accepting this as true in the abstract. They don't claim to be perfect or demand absolute infallibility from others.

And yet, one of the biggest sources of friction in a service relationship is when the servant honestly believes that their master is wrong about an order, or has a wrong perception that is negatively affecting the servant – or perhaps has a wrongheaded idea that has nothing to do with the servant, but simply knowing that the master holds this ridiculous idea damages their trust in their master in general. While there are a lot of ways to respectfully bring a potential error to a master's notice, and good masters will admit when they have actually been incorrect, sometimes it's a matter of world view or priorities. (We touch more on this problem in the chapter on Optimizing For Priorities.)

It's not uncommon for a servant to be faced with the dilemma of wanting to be right versus wanting to be obedient. However, it is something of an emotional catch-22: If the servant is continually right in a difference of opinion, this means that the master is continually wrong ... and this means that the master's judgment cannot be trusted, which means that the servant is not safe while following it. On the other hand, if the master is right ... well, the servant is wrong, and being wrong rankles most people. The choice is either to be unsafe or to be rankled, and the only good options are these:

1) Make a decision, once and for all, as to whether the master is actually so incompetent that following their orders at all times will cause someone serious harm. If this is really the case, you cannot serve them honorably, because they are not trustworthy.

2) If your decision is otherwise, focus on ways to *relax and let go*. One slave that we know has a mantra: "No one is going to die if I do things Master's way." Let go of the need to be right – because obedience is more important now. Let go of the worry and the need to be right. Let go of the responsibility. That's one of the perks of being on the bottom end, anyway – you're allowed to give it up and relax, and be carried along by the master's will.

It isn't necessary for the master to always be right, or for the servant to pretend the master was right when that is obviously not the case, but conflicts are resolved so much more smoothly if the servant genuinely wants the master's decision to turn out to be right. For example, it is easy for a servant to get stuck in an attitude of "I think you are wrong and I am right, and I don't think there is any way for you to convince me otherwise." It is radically different when the servant can reframe that feeling, and instead say to the master, "I don't understand how you could possibly be right on this, but maybe I'm missing something. Could you help me understand where you are coming from?"

Motivations for Service

Why bother to serve? Why do s-types do it? Besides, of course, "…because it's what subs/slaves do, so I'm doing it."? In watching and talking to s-types for many years, we've discerned that there seem to be three basic types of motivation for service. We're calling them Transactional, Devotional, and Positional, and we'll discuss each of them separately.

However, as you read this, it's important to keep in mind that each person is a complicated mix of motivations. Even if those motivations might fall into three categories, people don't. Our motivations may shift from person to situation to activity; we may manifest any of these at various times. These categories are presented so that people can have words for why they do things, and perhaps identify if one of these is more dominant than others in their personality.

Transactional Service

In transactional motivations for service, the individual is serving because they are getting a direct benefit from it. Ideally this is an exchange of equal value to them, or they would refuse to do it. The most obvious example of this is paid service – the cleaning lady and the waiter do their jobs because they are getting a paycheck at the end of the day. With unpaid situations, the exchange can be more or less overt or subtle; some people spell it all out in a contract, while for others it's just "assumed" that "I do this for you now because I know that you'll do that for me later, so it's worth it."

There are all sorts of reasons why people might consider service worth doing even if it isn't attractive on its own merits. A live-in houseboy or housemaid might clean the house because they're getting free rent and a certain amount of dominance from a trustworthy M-type. A part-time sub might fetch their dominant drinks at the bar because they know they're going to get some kinky action later, or because it adds to the fun of temporarily imagining themselves to be a slave, forced to serve or else something vague and terrible and titillating might happen. Another might serve because it gets them the appreciation of the people that they're serving, and they like to know that they can make a positive impact on the lives of others.

Every power dynamic should have at least a small amount of transactional motivation, because it keeps the servant in touch with their needs and whether those needs are actually getting met. If the servant is no longer getting what they need and what they believe that the master is obligated to give them, they'll become resentful and eventually leave. This is one reason why it's good to have largely transactional relationships clearly delineated; the master needs to know what the servant believes that they are supposed to be getting from them. Sometimes these relationships are built entirely on assumptions, and if those assumptions are not in line with each other, it will fail very quickly. Of course, this also means that the servant needs to be completely honest – not only with the master but with themselves as well – about what it is that they expect from the bargain. With straightforward honesty, this kind of service can work out very well in a long-distance relationship, or one where both parties can only see each other periodically, where the other motivations would be more painful and difficult.

One of the drawbacks to transactional service is that while it can work very well for short-term encounters, it's not so useful for long-term, 24/7, emotionally intimate relationships where boundaries can blur and "rewards" can get put off due to the vagaries of life interfering. The constant "accounting" gets tricky when it's every minute of every day, and sooner or later someone will start feeling shortchanged. Another drawback is that this motivation can only be pushed so far, as it is easily swayed by personal desires and selfishness. It's not necessarily the best foundation for a property-ownership situation, for example, or a no-recourse commitment where the slave is expected to be there permanently.

Devotional Service

Devotional motivations for service happen when the submissive serves out of love. It doesn't have to be romantic love – although it often is – but there is usually a feeling of "You are such a wonderful person that I am moved to do things for you, and I want very much to please you and to make you happy." Deep satisfaction is gained from helping the object of their warm feelings, in a way that wouldn't happen if they were rendering that service to some random person.

Love is an amazingly strong motivation, and can carry someone a long way in the face of difficulty. Therefore, this motivation lends itself best to long-term romantic relationships, and secondarily to relationships where the sub looks up to and admires the master as a person. There may also be a desire for the feeling of "belonging" – to a person, to a family, to a cause. Since devotional service is usually very one-pointed – "I serve you and no other!" – the master needs to be very careful about lending their servant to others. Long-distance relationships are the hardest for someone with this motivation, for obvious reasons.

The drawbacks to devotional service is that inevitably, a day will come when the servant doesn't feel all that loving, and may decide that service isn't being rendered on that day. We're all human, and eventually every couple – especially if they are living together – has a moment of "Damn it, today I just hate you!" Even if they get over it in a matter of hours, during that time their service will often be sabotaged by the lack of positive feelings. This can be particularly problematic with the combination of an emotionally volatile servant and "mission critical" tasks. A servant motivated primarily by devotion would do well to cultivate a little of the other two types of motivation to pull them through the "I hate you today" mornings.

Positional Service

Positional motivations for service come from the servant's strong sense of identity of themselves as a service-oriented person. They serve because it's part of who they are, and to refuse to serve would be to sabotage their own self-worth, which is often based on how well a job they do. Positionally-motivated servants take pride in serving as perfectly as possible, and they are the ones who get up to help because it needs doing, regardless of who is asking. They are the most likely to attempt to cultivate "pure" service, treating it as an art and requiring little in the way of appreciation. This category is the "ideal" slave in Laura Antoniou's fictional *Marketplace* series, where slaves are sold to random wealthy owners who may or may not be even remotely worthy as people, and the slaves are expected to serve their monied masters to the best of their ability anyway. As you might imagine, positionally-motivated servants do "lend out" quite well, should a master want such a thing.

Putting the chairs away after the BDSM potluck munch for the fiftieth time won't fly for the transactionally-motivated servant ("What's in it for me?") or the devotionally-motivated servant ("I don't love you; why should I do what you say?"), but the positionally-motivated servant will get up and do it anyway every time, because it's what they do. It is central to how they see themselves. However, one of the drawbacks to being a positionally-motivated servant is that their need to serve anyone, anything, for their own self-worth, can get them taken advantage of by unscrupulous people who want something for nothing.

Another drawback to this motivation is that it does tend to objectify dominants and perhaps see them as interchangeable. In contrast to the devotionally-motivated submissive who is fiercely bound to one particular person, the positionally-motivated servant may be happy to serve anyone for the sake of the service. Alongside the potential problems of choosing a less-than-worthy master, they might also irritate some dominants with their seeming lack of caring about whom they serve. Many dominants want to be seen as special, at least by their submissives, and they may be put off by the idea that they might as well be anyone else who would accept the submissive's service.

Adding a bit of devotion to the mix will help in that regard, and cultivating some transactional motivations will help to keep them from being taken advantage of too often.

Styles of Service

In this section, we aren't referring to "service roles", such as butler or houseboy or secretary or whore. We're talking about two different methods of giving service, which we refer to as "reactive service" and "proactive service".

Reactive service focuses on immediate obedience. The servant's job is to do exactly what they are told and no more than that, as quickly as possible. If they have not received a direct order to do it, they should not do it. If they haven't received any direct orders, they should be waiting patiently in lieu of standing orders. It is not their job to think ahead to the next possible order, or try to guess the master's bigger goal, or worry about any potential underlying subtle messages. Reactive service, at its plainest, is quite literal, although one of the pitfalls of doing nothing but reactive service for a long time can be the development of over-literality – "Which three eggs should I scramble, Mistress?"

This kind of service is most likely to be used in the beginning of a service relationship, because it allows the servant to learn the methods and preferences of the master while allowing them the smallest possible leeway to screw up. It's also good at training the servant's priorities. All too often, the servant will look at the master's methods and think to themselves, "I'd do it differently, and my way is better." We'll talk more about this pitfall later, but suffice it to say that a period of reactive service, where they are not given the chance – or even the situational temptation – to subtly insert their methods instead of the original orders, can help to break them of that mindset.

Reactive service is on a continuum with proactive service on the other end. Proactive service can happen once a servant is familiar with the master's methods, preferences, and general way of moving through the world. Ideally, they would not only have internalized all standing orders, but would have developed a little "master puppet" in their head who would tell them whether a given action would be approved of. They need to have an invisible version of those letter bracelets, one which says WWMW – "What Would Master Want?" They also need to have internalized the reality of their situation to the point where they would not be inserting their own desires and priorities and telling themselves that this is what the master would want ... if he/she were sensible, of course.

While reactive service is done primarily in response to immediate and direct orders, proactive service is more frequently done in response to standing orders. The servant may go through their daily routine without the master's presence at all, following the trail that has been laid out for them, and that they understand thoroughly. If a situation comes up for which they have no standing orders, they should be able to extrapolate what the master would want them to do, and make good decisions on the matter. It puts the servant on a much longer leash, and requires the master to trust them a lot more than the supervised results of reactive service.

Sometimes the master may have a firm big-picture goal but doesn't particularly care about the details – and in fact expects that having a competent servant will mean that they can continue to ignore those details. For example: "I want a well-maintained car that runs, and when it ceases to run for whatever reason, I want it to start running again as soon as possible, and I want alternate transportation to appear in the meantime. Here's the budget I have for that; if that's not sufficient, you can talk to me about it. Otherwise, I don't want to have to worry about it." Housework may be another area where this approach is common. This puts a great deal of responsibility on the servant, and assumes that they have the knowledge and skills to make it happen.

At the high end of proactive service we have "anticipatory service", where the servant tries to guess what the master would want before the master even thinks of it themselves, and have it ready to pleasantly surprise them. This requires lengthy observation of the master and their lifestyle, and good psychological skills – especially involving "theory of mind" – in order to pull off properly. There are many warning tales circulating about servants who tried anticipatory service before they deeply understood the master's preferences and priorities, and presented the master with a *fait accompli* that the master hated. Even worse, some of them took it personally and became upset when their error was rejected. The servant who experiments with anticipatory service – assuming that their master wants that sort of thing – should learn to take rejections gracefully and not inadvertently penalize the master for the crime of not wanting the unsolicited service they have offered.

Masters have widely differing desires when it comes to reactive and proactive service, and especially anticipatory service. This may be due to their specific styles of dominance – which we discuss in the next section – but in general, some masters love proactive service because it's less work for them, and find anticipatory service luxurious and delightful. They love it when things happen "automagically". Others dislike proactive service and may especially dislike anticipatory service, either because they've had it go wrong too many times and they don't trust the servant to get it right, or because part of their joy in the power dynamic is hands-on, up-close control over the servant, and they would rather be directly involved in most or all of the orders. Masters will usually make it very clear when they don't want proactive service, or when they want the servant to be reactive in some areas but proactive in others. ("I expect you to take care of the household chores yourself, but when it comes to the cooking, you're just going to chop what I tell you and sauté what I tell you and don't worry about the rest of it.") If they aren't clear about the orders for whatever reason, the servant should respectfully ask for clarification before they make a mistake.

Styles of Dominance

Dominants (and we are temporarily including masters, mistresses, owners, and all the other People In Charge under this umbrella for the purposes of this chapter) are all very different folks. Unlike the porn stereotypes which would have them all put into the same "Fetch me a drink, slave!" category, they have varying attitudes toward service. For some, it's important to their daily comfort. For others, it's merely a way to assert their dominance. For yet others, it's not important at all. Some are micromanagers who want to be as hands-on as possible; some want to be able to wave a hand at their majordomo-slave and say, "Make it so."

From interviewing and watching various M-types in the demographic, we've noticed a continuum of dominant styles. Some are firmly at one end or the other, while others may shift from day to day, or activity to activity, or slowly over a lifetime. Many are somewhere in the middle. We've decided to refer to one end as "parental" dominance, and the other as "celebrity" dominance, and they shape what kind of service an s-type will be allowed to give.

Here's an example of the far ends of the spectrum: Two M/s couples walk into a restaurant. (No, this is not the start of a bad joke.) The first couple pull up in a car driven by the master, because the slave isn't allowed to drive, and might not even have been informed of where they were going. After being seated, the master takes both menus and orders for both of them, because the master knows what's best for the slave to eat. The master decides when they are finished, and pays the bill because there's no need for the slave to handle money.

The second couple pulls up in a car driven by the slave, who is the chauffeur. While the master make a cell phone call in the parking lot, the slave goes in and gets a table by the window, because that is where the master likes to sit. The slave orders for both of them, because the slave has been briefed in exactly what the master wants, and the idea is to have the favorite meal ready when they come in. The master finishes chatting and comes to the table shortly before the food arrives. After they are finished eating, the master breezes out while the slave calculates the tip and takes care of paying the bill, because the master has better things to do than to be bothered with such annoyances.

Two couples, two styles which are both entirely legitimate – and probably much loved by some couples out there. While most may be somewhere in the middle, they probably have occasional moments of one extreme or the other. Think of them as the X axis and Y axis of dominance, and you can plot your point on a mental graph, or that of your favorite M-type. Let's look at them a little more closely:

Parental Dominance

We're using the word "parental" here, but we definitely aren't referring to any sort of ageplay. We also aren't implying that the submissive should be considered anything other than an adult. However, the amount of hands-on management is very similar to what is required to parent a child. This is a high-control style; at the far end of the continuum, the dominant may control very personal aspects of the slave's life – their clothing, hairstyle, diet, exercise, daily schedule, bedtime, orgasms, money, etc.

If these are the X and Y "axes" of dominance, then control and service are two of the main "axes" of the power dynamic itself. Some people crave controlling or being controlled more, while some crave service or being served. However, almost all power dynamics manifest some form of both. While the "parental dynamic" may look like total control, there are often various forms of service going on. They may be for more traditional reasons of wanting to be served, or they may just be ways that the master reifies their dominance by making the slave do things for them. Either way, it's likely to be reactive service – a very controlled and possibly micromanaged "Do as I say." The biggest service rendered by the submissive is simply being completely obedient in the moment to whatever they are told.

It's important to have a good fit along these axes if a power dynamic relationship is to survive. A strongly service-oriented submissive who prefer proactive service and prides themselves on being able to anticipate their dominant's needs will be unhappy and frustrated with an extreme parental style. "What, do you think I'm that incompetent? Why don't you let me use my skills for you?" they will wonder, and it may eventually have a negative impact on their self-esteem. If there is also, as there often is, an element of controlling behavior that periodically sets them up to fail – either for the master's entertainment or to teach them not to do more than react without much thinking – then they may feel even more like a constant failure. At best, they may achieve a kind of epiphany where they realize that the best service they can provide is to learn to be constantly in a kind of serene meditative "living in the now" state. However, it sometimes happens that a submissive in this state does not provide enough emotional reaction for the control-oriented dominant, so they end up failing anyway.

Celebrity Dominance

Think Batman and his own batman, Alfred! The celebrity dominant wants the obstacles smoothed out of their path, and while there is probably extensive training to familiarize the submissive with all the dominant's preferences, the end goal may be a dynamic of almost complete service with very little hands-on control. While some celebrity dominants may not actually do anything more important than holding a day job and watching TV, this is often a style of dominance preferred by hard-driving career people with complicated lives who want the ultimate perfectly obedient Man or Girl Friday to take care of the smaller details. The submissive may be expected to learn a wide variety of skills and take on tasks with very little supervision. They may function as a personal assistant, personal care attendant, and/or extra unpaid employee for a business. They might be a majordomo, managing a household and possibly a staff of other slaves or hired help. Their job is to "take care of it," whatever "it" is, and to make the dominant feel as pampered as they might like.

This is a dynamic where proactive service is required, and possibly even a high level of anticipatory service. Again, a poor fit is a problem. Control-oriented submissives who prefer reactive service may feel like they're being abandoned and told to "master themselves". They pine for lack of attention and the feel of the master's direct will, and may eventually accuse them of "not really being dominant." They may feel like they are being used, more of a maid than a partner in a power dynamic, and may feel that their opposite number is shirking their responsibility. All too often, they get desperate for any kind of attention and act out with obvious disobedience, hoping for the crackdown and the strong hand. The celebrity dominant generally feels that this is wasting their limited time, and won't keep them around very long.

The servant who is right for a celebrity dominant is generally one who is strongly invested in their own feelings of competence, and enjoys taking on responsibility. They tend to be more interested in service than control, or perhaps they get their control fix from the bedroom or less day-to-day parts of the relationship. They are comfortable with proactive service and perhaps even anticipatory service. It's also often someone who is invested in the life and work of that particular M-type, and part of their surrender is becoming subsumed into that life and work, skills and all. They may enjoy being an integral part of something bigger than them, and they may take pride in being good enough at their job to be indispensable.

The Annoyance Factor

(This chapter is written specifically and entirely by Raven, as it is a chronicle of his struggles with managing a slave. It is, therefore, written entirely in the first person singular, unlike the rest of this book, which was a collaborative effort.)

When we first started out together in our M/s relationship, the hardest part of all for me was remembering to enforce the orders I'd given. Joshua was extremely obedient – fortunately – but he would often forget to do what I'd asked, and if I didn't check up on whether it was done, he'd continue to forget and it would never develop into a habit. Sometimes we'd both forget and then one of us would remember days or weeks later—and then he'd be upset both with himself for forgetting, and with me for not noticing. We went through a lot of orders and protocols that way, orders and protocols that just weren't going to work. I had a busy life and I couldn't always keep track of it all, and neither could he.

Later, we'd learn that this was one of the most common early mistakes of service-oriented power dynamic relationships. M-types start out with an idealistic list of activities that they'd like their s-types to do for them, but many of them aren't practical for the fit of their daily lives, and the amount of time and attention they actually have available to spend enforcing them. This is especially difficult when first constructing a full-time 24/7 dynamic where there are no periods of "on" and "off". It is definitely the M-type's responsibility to do the checking up, assessing, and enforcing – it's the other side of the coin, the price we pay for all that obedience and service – but we also have a responsibility to ourselves to choose those orders sensibly.

This mistake is especially common when people are transitioning from a part-time, scene-oriented relationship to a full-time, live-in dynamic. By their nature, part-time relationships are concentrated periods of super-D/s. The people involved try to pack a whole lot into a short time, and then they go home to their "regular" lives. That kind of concentrated focus on the details of the dynamic feels great for a weekend, but when it gets stretched over all the pieces in between that were formerly "regular time", it often becomes clear that it's impossible to keep up that kind of focus. This isn't a failing – it's a reality. Couples who are making this kind of transition may well need to back up and start over, rather than just trying to adapt a periodic pattern to every day.

Eventually – and please understand that this process took a couple of years – I gave up and threw out all the failing protocols, and started over. I looked at the ones that were left – the ones that I'd consistently been able to notice and check up on – and figured out what they had in common. For every one of them, *their lack of appearance created an immediate annoyance for me.* For example, Joshua is my chauffeur and drives me around. When I walk over the passenger side of the door, it's supposed to be unlocked – he is supposed to get there before me and open it. Every time that I got to my door and couldn't open it, I had a surge of annoyance and would immediately call his omission to his attention, often loudly. Similarly, he is also supposed to report to me as soon as he gets home, given the few minutes it takes to drop off groceries in the kitchen, navigate around the dog, etc. When I hear our car pull into the driveway and the front door slam, I immediately become vigilant for his arrival to kneel at my feet. Whenever it didn't happen within a few minutes, I would become displeased and go to look for him.

Starting with these as a basis, I began to look around for the other annoying things in my life – things that I would love to see disappear, and would definitely find unpleasant were they to suddenly appear again. Some of these could readily be taken over by Joshua so as to spare me the annoyance, and I found that they were easily noticed and corrected when he forgot them. I also took a long and honest look at each of the protocols I'd assigned because I thought that they would be cool, or sexy, or particularly master-slavey. A disconcertingly high number of them turned out to not have enough deep significance, when push came to shove, for me to notice when they fell away. They just weren't as pleasurable to me as I'd hoped that they would be. A few stayed; his "Thank you, sir," after each orgasm that he was allowed to have or allowed to give me, for example. An omission of that and a few other similar protocols was glaringly obvious, not because of inconvenience, but because I loved to hear it and it reified our dynamic for me. However, many of the protocols that I'd read about in BDSM erotica or Old Guard-style manuals *looked* good, but didn't carry enough of a charge for me in the end.

In some cases, the impetus for the psychological protocol had come from him. He found some activity arousing or deeply meaningful, and I agreed both because I wanted to make him happy – because I do care about his happiness in this job – and because I thought that some activities that he particularly liked would be good for his morale. It was hard for both of us to accept that I just couldn't find the internal motivation to continually pay attention to protocols that did nothing for me. The ones that worked were based around my own selfishness – my convenience, my annoyance, my hard-on, my emotional responses. Faced with his disappointment, I had two choices: I could beat myself up for not being able to do this, or we could work together on making the activities that were meaningful for me likewise meaningful for him. We chose the second option, and it has worked out well. It wasn't even that difficult. It was simply a matter of communicating clearly, every time I reinforced one of the activities that was meaningful to me, that this was yet another way in which I showed my power over him ... and in some cases, yet another way in which he rendered me service, if only by enduring what I wanted. Eventually, every one of these things became meaningful for him as well, through repetition and seeing that it pleased me.

I also enlisted Joshua's help in discovering new and unusual ways in which he could render me service, derived from his keen and constant observation of my life. Sometimes his suggestions were excellent; sometimes they simply weren't something I was interested in. An example of one brilliant idea was ordering in restaurants. Some dominants order the food for their submissives in order to show dominance or hold them to a specific diet; that never interested me, and I would generally ignore whatever he wanted to eat. I, on the other hand, am one of those people who finds that their normal decisive nature completely vacates the premises when faced with a food menu. Seeing me struggle, he suggested that paring the possibilities down to two was easier than choosing only one, and offered me his food choice as a service. I could order the two most likely-looking meals and he would either eat the one that proved less desirable, or let me eat from both and finish off the remainder. There was no way that I would forget to enforce this one, as it alleviated a good deal of stress every time I faced down a new menu.

The biggest lesson that we learned from this was that it's better to have only a few rules, protocols, and delineated services – and be able to keep track of every one, remember to enforce them, and have the servant work on perfecting their delivery – than to have a whole lot of rules to which both parties can only give a half-assed amount of attention. We also learned that if we're going to add a rule, protocol, or service that is untested, and might or might not pass the bar of the annoyance factor for me, it's best to add only one at a time. Once we've determined whether it's going to be permanent or not, we can try another, but until then we just work on one. It keeps frustrations and disappointments to a minimum, on both sides of the relationship.

It's often best if both parties try hard not to get strongly invested in any new protocol when it's still in the experimental stage. It might not work out, and that doesn't mean that either or both of you have failed, or that whoever came up with it was an idiot. If you can both go into the process of adding protocols with an attitude of "It'd be nice if this works, but if it doesn't it's no big deal," it will make things much easier on the self-esteem of both parties, and their faith in the dynamic will not be dented as easily. Remember that this is a custom-fitted relationship, and all custom-fittings take time. There isn't anyone watching and judging you on how numerous or master-slavey your protocols are – and if there is, tell them to go away and mind their own business!

Optimizing for Priorities

Priorities are the source of many arguments and misunderstandings between masters and servants. It was an "aha!" moment for Joshua when he finally figured out that when he and Raven disagreed on how a job should be done, it was because they were optimizing for different priorities. One of the triggers for that moment was when Joshua asked Raven why he carried the laundry out the front door and all the way around the house to the line, instead of going out the back door which was much closer. Raven answered, "Because I hate hanging the laundry, and walking through my beautiful herb garden on the way there helps motivate me to do it." Joshua was optimizing for efficiency; Raven was optimizing for pleasure.

Sometimes the servant is focused on absolute efficiency and the master wants to do it the way that makes them feel the best. Sometimes the master is focused on absolute efficiency and the servant wants to do it the way that makes them feel the most "slavey". Sometimes one of them is relying on an archetype of "how these things should be done" and the other is looking at what would be more useful for the actual situation. Sometimes both are prioritizing for different sets of equally irrational cultural values or avoidance of psychological triggers.

What's the answer when this happens? It's both easy and terribly hard: the master's priorities win every time. While the master might choose to take the servant's ideas into consideration, and might even change their minds if they think the ideas are good enough, they are not obligated to do so. The servant is obligated to do things the master's way, and if they're a good servant, they should work on not acting too resentful while they're doing it. A good thought process to focus on during those trying times might be, "I'm serving this person because I believe they're worthy of it. Their way makes sense from their perspective, given who they are and how their mind works. If I trust that person and that mind, I can do it their way."

Another even simpler one might be "No one is going to die if I do things Master's way."

The issue of priorities is one that generally comes up more fully in a slightly later stage of relationship development. This is because of the necessary order of give-and-take required by a deeply and consciously inegalitarian relationship. It's necessary for the M-type to earn the s-type's trust first, and that's the way that it has to be, because they are so vulnerable. The M-type has to prove to the s-type that they really do want complete honesty (and possibly transparency, depending on their negotiated dynamic) and in order to do that, they have to meet every "unacceptable" honest thought the s-type hesitantly communicates to them with calm, non-defensive assurance, no matter what they are actually feeling. This process may take months or years. After it's done, they can decide if they want to give the s-type the privilege of actually seeing their emotions in the moment, and actually seeing the process by which they decide their priorities.

It is very much an act of great trust for the M-type to pull the curtain aside and fully show their intimate selves, and it's important that the s-type understands that seeing their process is a privilege that must be earned, just as their own trust was earned. The relationship has to evolve to a certain maturity first, and the s-type has to prove that they are going to meet the unveiling of this process with the kind of forbearance that the M-type showed for their honesty. If the M-type's priorities are occasionally unflattering in situations with difficult choices, they will be depending on the s-type's discretion. If the s-type doesn't like their priorities, attempts by the s-type to change them is not only inappropriate to their position but probably futile. The servant's choices are to adapt – which can include asking the M-type to help them find a way to adapt – or decide that they need to find someone whose priorities are a better fit.

For Masters: Integrating the Servant Into the Routine

When we talk about service that isn't just sexual or fetish, some masters become a bit squirrelly. They don't want service, they tell me, because they pride themselves on being self-sufficient and they don't need the slave to do anything for them. Sometimes there's an underlying feeling of "I don't want to become dependent on anyone for anything," which is its own kind of insecurity. Assuming that the power in a relationship belongs to whoever is less invested is a big mistake, as experienced masters and mistresses will tell you. However, sometimes the objection is more pragmatic. "But I like cooking and doing the laundry. Why should I give that away to my slave?" In some cases they tell me, "I'm a better cook (or auto mechanic or whatever) than my slave. Why shouldn't I be the one to do it?"

The answer is: If you want to be the one to do it, of course you should be the one to do it. If there are certain chores that you love and that you're good at, by all means do them. However, even the most beloved of chores may have little fiddly parts that you'd rather not bother with, and that can be handled by a slave, thus giving you a more enjoyable experience. You're a great chef and you like to do the cooking … but do you really want to chop every little piece of garlic yourself, grease pans, whip interminable amounts of egg white, or stop in the middle to wash up that big bowl? You like to do the laundry … but do you like running downstairs halfway through the cycle to put in the softener? You want to vacuum the carpets yourself … but do you want to have your flow impeded by stopping to move the furniture around? You want to do the taxes yourself … but do you want to waste your time calling up those credit card accounts to figure out what sort of forgotten purchases were made? You want to change the oil in the car … but do you want to haul yourself out from underneath halfway through because you forgot the right wrench?

There are useful ways to integrate a servant into your routine, ways to ensure that you work together as a team and not at cross-purposes. First, go through your usual tasks with extra mindfulness. Take note of every time you sigh in frustration because some small boring part of the process isn't as fun as the rest of it, or when it would go faster if you had two sets of hands. If you have a good servant, you have that. Use them for the bits that you wish could just happen "automagically", if they can be trained to do them properly (and often those bits aren't the parts that require great skill, just attention, conscientiousness, and the willingness to do boring, repetitive labor).

Second, visualize adapting the slave to fit in with the routine. Do they have the requisite skill and patience already, or would they require extensive training? Should you order them to come into the process partway through, or should they be observing and jump in at a pre-arranged "cue"? Would their contribution be time-sensitive? How will they adapt to that? It's useful to walk through it in your head before walking them through it, because it means less dithering during the actual training.

There's another good reason that you should integrate them into the work process: it will give them a close-up, hands-on experience of how you like things done. Many servants are very set in their ways when it comes to how certain tasks – especially household ones – should be done. They may have trouble getting over their ideas in favor of yours. ("But Mistress, it's so much more *efficient* if you do it this way!") This is an error on their part; it's not their job to change your process or find a better one. It's their job to learn to do things the way that you want them done.

Third, begin to slowly integrate them into the process. There can be a good deal of trial and error in this, and the best method is to be patient. If you give them a piece of the process and then later decide that you want it back, it's all right to change your mind. It's also all right to keep them hanging around doing very little, just in case you need them for something. You don't need to feel obligated to find something for them to do right then just because they're bored. It may be irritating to them, but it's part of the process that can't be rushed. A little waiting around in the beginning is worth it for everyone to know what is expected of them. If, after thorough consideration of the situation, you really can't find any way for them to actually benefit you by their involvement, set the idea aside for now. Maybe at some time in the future an idea might come to you.

If they need training in skills or information in order to help effectively, this doesn't necessarily need to be hugely time-consuming for you. For example, if you want the servant to be able to get you supplies or equipment while you work, they need to be able to accurately identify those items and locate them reasonably quickly. You can go over the names and locations of the most commonly used items while the servant takes notes (or perhaps photos) to study on their own. Especially if they do not live with you, it can be very effective to assign them skills to practice, or techniques to research and learn on their own. However, some people enjoy taking a very hands-on approach to training, and might make a game out of testing their servant's new knowledge, incorporating rewards, punishments, or "funishments" based on their performance.

Don't feel obligated to let them reorganize your tools or modify your process right away. It is common for some servants to approach this sort of work with a stance of, "I can't possibly help you unless you change to accommodate me." While this might be true to some extent, it can set up an unhealthy pattern, so you if you have a pushy or opinionated servant you may want to be very conservative in how much input you allow them to have in the process. With some servants, it can be very effective to eventually allow them to reorganize your tools as a reward for them achieving a certain level of competency in assisting, and in this context it reinforces the power dynamic, rather than positioning them as someone who is compensating for your failings.

We are assuming, in this book, that the tasks you will give to your servant are real jobs that actually need doing, and that you have a vested interest in the results being satisfactory. This means that you need to give accurate feedback, and they need to be able to hear the feedback and take it graciously. A good servant sees criticism as useful information that will help them to do a better job. Make it clear that during this process, you will critique their performance, but you're doing it as a way to get them to where you want them more quickly. Reinforce the idea that feedback shows that you actually care about how they're doing, and aren't just settling for the less-than-optimal job which is all you think they're capable of. Putting it this way can put an entirely different spin on criticism for all but the most insecure servants.

So far we've emphasized that you should be teaching them your way rather than asking them for their input. The sole exception to this might be if you asked them to find you a better way to do something, and if that's the case, they should be designing that better way with you and your satisfaction in mind. In order to do that skillfully, they need to log many hours of watching you work and solve problems; otherwise it will simply be the solution that works for them, not the one that works for you. If they aren't sure, their best bet is to bring you more than one "formal proposal" and let you decide which one suits you best. If they tend toward bossiness, but you want their input anyway, it can help to make them offer the proposal in a format that you are more comfortable with than they are. This interrupts the habitual "bossy" behavior and gives them the opportunity to develop a more service-oriented way of expressing their suggestions.

In these situations, there is often a great deal of temptation to slant things toward the process that they feel is the most correct, or that makes their job easier or more interesting, rather than the one that will satisfy you the most.

The best way to handle this is a continual and consistent policy of positive reinforcement for honesty and negative reinforcement for white lies in the rest of the relationship. This includes the times when their honesty is difficult for you to hear and you must respond calmly and gracefully to it anyway. Be a role model for not using the dynamic to coddle your pride, and point out to them where the standard goes both ways.

For Servants: Minimally Invasive Organizing

In general, this book suggests specific services a person might provide but does not describe in detail how to provide those services. There are no recipes, no tips on natural cleansers, and no advice on making the perfect pot of tea. If a servant is genuinely interested in learning how to be a better cook, housekeeper, handyman, or secretary, they ought to be able to find information on how to do that without someone spoon-feeding it to them. However, we decided that it was important for Joshua to describe his approach to organizing in a fair amount of detail. Not only is it a skill that many people find useful, but it provides an example of how the servant can render a service in accordance with the master's preferences, while maintaining an attitude appropriate to their role.

Masters who are very organized generally have no trouble instructing the servant in their methods, but the less organized master is often unsure of how to proceed if a servant suggests organizing their space. If the master feels guilty about their own lack of organizational skills, they may allow the servant to change their space in ways that don't work for them, or they may be reluctant to set firm boundaries about what the servant is and is not permitted to organize. If the servant is the primary person using the space, then it makes sense to let them organize it however they like, but if the master uses the space in any significant way, it is best for the master to insist that the space be organized in a way that suits them.

There are countless sources for advice on organizing a space, but most of them are based on the idea that the person whose space is being organized wants to be part of the organizational effort and is willing to substantially change their routine. They also tend to assume that for household organizing, the person doing the organizing (i.e. "Mom") has the right to attempt to change the behavior of other members of the household. Joshua's approach is based on disrupting the master's routine as little as possible, and organizing in ways that make use of the master's natural tendencies.

This is the basic process for the servant to follow:

1. Observe the way the master uses the space. What items do they use frequently? What items do they use together? What items do they need to be able to access in a hurry? What items do they never use? What items have they bought replacements for because they couldn't find the ones they already had?

2. Talk to the master about their personal preferences. Do they like certain things to remain in plain sight? Do they like complex storage boxes with lots of little compartments? Do they want storage containers to be decorative? Do they value a highly flexible, adaptable system? Do they like things thoroughly labeled, alphabetized, and color-coded, or does that seem excessively anal-retentive to them? Do they enjoy browsing through a selection of items to find the right item, or do they generally know exactly what item they want? How much money are they willing to spend on organizational supplies? Are they looking for a radical change in the space, or would they be more comfortable with a few small changes to start out?

> Under no circumstances is it appropriate for a servant to dispose of items the master would have chosen to keep, even if they are certain the master won't ever miss it. Even if the disposed items are grubby unmatched Tupperware, it is still a huge breach of the trust a master places in a servant who is charged with stewarding the master's possessions.

3. Determine whether the master is interested in getting rid of unused items. If they are, should the items be thrown away, given to charity, sold, or disposed of otherwise? If they are not, then drop the issue without argument or further discussion. If the master expresses reluctance to allow the servant to get rid of anything, the servant should not push the issue. Aside from being inappropriate, obtaining a grudging agreement to purge items will frequently result in a time-consuming and aggravating struggle over every other item

selected for disposal, on the grounds that it has sentimental value or that they "might need it one day". It is far better to simply pack up the unused items and store them in a safe, out-of-the-way location, and reassess the situation the next time the area is organized.

4. Figure out categories that fit with the master's way of working and their way of thinking. Don't try to impose categories that don't make sense to them. Before you get too deep into the process, tell them your general idea and see if they like it. If they have ideas about categorization, use those ideas to the fullest extent practical. You don't need to agree with their categorization, or understand why it works for them, but ideally you should be able to figure out how to categorize an item according to their "system".

5. When determining where to store an item, keep in mind the way it is used. For example, you may want to consider the following:

> ✷ Items used frequently should very easy to access. If space is limited, put the items the master uses in the most easily accessible locations, and use the less convenient storage areas for your own things. If there are any items which the master would like immediate access to, these should be put in a readily accessible locations, even if they are rarely used.

> ✷ Items used with each other or for the same purpose should be stored together whenever possible, and ideally near the place where they are most often used. If an inexpensive item is used in multiple different contexts, getting duplicate items can greatly simplify the task.

> ✷ Items which tend to be "browsed" should be stored in a way that permits this. That is, if people frequently know they want an item of that type, but aren't sure exactly which one they want, or aren't sure what is currently available, they should be able to easily see their options. (This is common with food, clothing, books, and many hobby items.)

7. Reduce the effort required of them to maintain organization. It is common for masters to be much more

resistant to change than their servants, and much less inclined to do things the way they are told to do them. The ideal is to make it the established location for an item the easiest and most obvious place to put it. Clearly labeled drawers and containers are generally highly effective. Masters (and other members of the household) are generally much more inclined to leave an item laying in plain sight than to stick it into a container clearly labeled for another purpose. Don't discourage this! It is far easier to put an item away yourself than it is to try to figure out weeks later where your master might have stashed it. Also, clear labeling reduces instances of the master feeling like the servant has "hidden" their things.

> Remember the first rule of service: *If the master doesn't want it, it isn't service.* If the master doesn't feel they've gotten substantial benefit from an organizational system, they will eventually decide the servant's time is better spent elsewhere. If the servant finds the system beneficial to their own work, they can explain this to the master, but this is rarely persuasive unless the time and effort to maintain the system is minimal and any time-intensive organizing is done during the servant's "free time".

8. After the new system is in place, observe how the space is being used, and assess whether the organizational strategies seem effective. If people are not using the space in the way you had hoped, it may be appropriate to offer gentle reminder of the intended system, but it is not appropriate (or generally effective) to insist anyone in the household do things a certain way. The servant's job is to simply observe, and if necessary revise the system.

9. Any organizational system requires periodic maintenance. An effective and appropriate system should not require a huge amount of time or effort to maintain, but the servant should periodically verify that various things are where they ought to be, and that any changes that have occurred since the last organizational effort are being well accommodated by the system.

Major organizational efforts should generally be undertaken only after the servant has demonstrated their ability to act in accordance with the master's preferences rather than their own. In situations where the master is very eager to make use of a new servant's organizational skills, the master should be especially careful that the servant maintains an attitude appropriate for their role, and defers without argument to the master's preferences. Well-organized people frequently feel a strong sense of superiority towards disorganized people, and confronting this attitude is essential for establishing a healthy and respectful service relationship.

It can be beneficial for the servant to use neutral non-judgmental language when discussing organizational issues. For example, referring to the "established location" of an item, rather than the "right place" or the "wrong place", and saying something like "I would expect that item to be..." rather than "That item *should* be..." In general, it is corrosive to the relationship to put the servant in a position where they are continually telling the master what to do or the way things ought to be. It can also be beneficial to strictly enforce a ban on anything resembling "nagging", including arguments about whether a given statement constitutes "nagging".

If a master decides they are not interested in allowing their servant to organize their space, they have no obligation to humor the organizationally-inclined servant. However, it is worthwhile to note that some masters are habitually disorganized because they associate a well-organized space with an authority figure telling them to clean up or else. If the master has a strong emotional reaction to the idea of organization, but would like to be able to find and use certain items more easily, they might find it useful to allow a trusted servant to organize one small area, using a minimally invasive approach. It is best to select an area where the disorder is especially annoying to the master, but not an area where the master has strong emotional attachment to the items. If the master finds benefit in the newly organized space, they can gradually allow the servant to organize other spaces, but the servant should be very careful to maintain the minimally invasive approach and not pressure the master about the issue.

Correcting Problematic Behavior

In this book, we've focused on what we call "real service", meaning that these are real-world ways in which one person can make the life of another more comfortable. In a very real way, this kind of service passes from the realm of "play" to the realm of "work". The servant is no longer playing with the master, but working for them. Because of this, the issue of obedience takes on a whole new dimension. If an s-type forgets to use an honorific or sits on unauthorized furniture, no real harm is done to a person or a household. If they decide not to pick up the dry cleaning or the children, leave the dog unsupervised in the kitchen, mouth off at the master's new client, misplace the master's medication, or wreck the car, there are real-world consequences beyond the master's displeasure. When you deal with real service, you require real obedience.

Obviously, nobody is perfect. In most situations, the occasional mistake is to be expected, especially when people are operating close to the edge of their competency. A master should quickly establish with the servant what the acceptable margin of error is for various tasks, and ensure the servant's skill and training is sufficient to reliably achieve that.

We tend to assume that servants are responsible adults who want to do a good job, and will sincerely apply themselves to the tasks assigned to them. A responsible servant does what their

It takes a certain temperament in a servant to consistently operate close to the edge of their competency or on an extremely narrow margin of error. A master who desires that of a servant would do well to select one with a personal or family background in military service, law enforcement, emergency medicine, firefighting, or any other situation where mistakes mean that people die. It is difficult (though not impossible) for a master to develop this temperament in a servant who has never been exposed to this level of real-world consequences.

master tells them to do, because it is their job. In our experience, the s-types who make the best servants do not respond well to traditional "punishment" as a correction method. The only situation where we feel any type of physical correction might be useful for some s-types is as an instantaneous response to a specific habitual behavior that has not responded to correction by other means, as a form of operant conditioning. However, all s-types are different, and masters have their own opinions and methods, so your mileage may vary.

The method that we find most effective is to set clear expectations and to work with the s-type to find a way for them to meet those expectations. We feel it is essential to make it clear to the s-type that they have an obligation to actively work toward changing their behavior, just as the master has an obligation to help them in that task. Masters and servants should be on the same team, not adversaries.

This is our basic method for addressing most problems:

1) **Bring the servant's attention to the situation, and verify that they understand what the problem is.**

The first time a problem occurs, it may be sufficient for the master to clarify their expectations and ensure the servant understands. With an experienced servant, the master often only needs to give a general indication that something about the situation is not up to the usual standard – many masters can do this with nothing more than a raised eyebrow – and the servant can immediately recognize the problem and take steps to correct it. An inexperienced servant may need a more explicit description of what they did wrong, and what is expected of them.

2) **Determine why the problem occurred.**

With a good servant, it is generally just an honest mistake, and all that is needed is the assurance that the servant will endeavor to avoid that mistake in the future. In cases where there were unforeseen or unusual circumstances, it may be beneficial to clarify what the appropriate response would have been in that situation, or what steps could have been taken to prevent that situation from arising.

An inexperienced servant may not be able to give any meaningful answer when questioned about what happened. They may be very emotionally distressed or confrontational. They may think that the only response appropriate to their role is hysterical groveling, or they may be very resistant to the idea that their transgression is going to be met with reasonable discussion, rather than yelling and punishment. Whether they are stuck in a fantasy role, acting out their dysfunctional upbringing, or just extremely emotionally sensitive, it is useful to discuss exactly what went wrong, and what factors contributed to that.

If the servant deliberately went against orders, in a way that was not justified by situation, this is a serious behavioral problem, no matter how trivial the order.

3) Develop a plan for preventing this problem in the future.

If having the servant try harder isn't producing the desired results, the next step is for both master and servant to look at the situation in detail, and "brainstorm" ideas about how to do things differently in the future. The master evaluates these ideas and decides on a plan, and both work together to implement that plan. Some examples of solutions might be: finding memory aids, dealing with underlying insecurities, working on the servant being mindful of their health, training them to ask for what they want, or

In many situations, failure comes from simple, preventable errors rather than unforeseeable circumstances or a lack of skill. If this is the case, consider making a list of the commonly overlooked steps, to be read and verified by the servant before completing the task. It may seem excessively rigid or limiting to reduce a complex task to a checklist, but by reliably removing obvious sources of error, a person can devote their full attention to the more complex aspects of the work, and consistently perform to a much higher standard.

even finding them external therapy. Getting the servant involved with finding solutions, and making it clear that results are the ultimate goal, helps to make them more invested in making the solution successful.

4) If necessary, reevaluate the servant's capabilities.

Everyone has different skills and strengths, and everyone has things they aren't very good at. If after diligent effort, the servant is still not able to consistently perform to the given standard in an area of service, the master may need to reevaluate whether this person is capable of the task, or reevaluate their standard. (If the master feels the servant is not applying themselves or is trying to avoid work, this is a serious behavioral problem, addressed in the section below.)

We have found that for an otherwise good servant, the most effective approach to persistent failures is for the master to drastically reduce their expectations of the servant's competence in the area, and then slowly build back up from there. The master begins by making the task excruciatingly simple, and moves on to more complex tasks only when the simple tasks have been mastered so thoroughly that the servant is sick of them. This approach works well for many different types of servants. When done in a supportive way, it can give the emotionally sensitive servant an opportunity to develop confidence in their skills without (realistic) fear of failure. For less emotionally sensitive servants, mild humiliation can be incorporated, especially if the initial attempts are unsuccessful. (Think of techniques that might be used to assist a small child in doing the task.) For example, we spoke to one servant who continually forgot orders. He was given a small notebook to carry with him at all times, and told to write down every single order he received. When he then forgot to bring the notebook, he was made to wear it on a string around his neck. This technique is especially effective for the stubborn servant who responds to their failure with, "See! I *told* you I was no good at that." It uses their natural "I'll show you!" response to the master's benefit. Finally, if the servant's failure is in any part motivated by a desire to avoid being assigned the task in the future, they may be inclined to try harder if failure results in tedious practice of the same task until they get it right.

Remedial Obedience

With a good servant, and reasonable expectations from the master, there is no need for specific obedience training. However, there are some s-types who could make good servants, but need some help to get to a point where they can consistently perform to a reasonable standard. Some are very attached to a fantasy role, but otherwise suitable. Some have bad habits from past relationships or dysfunctional upbringing. Some still have a bit of growing up to do, no matter what their chronological age is. Some have appallingly poor self-control.

> Evaluating a servant's work history gives the master an idea about the servant's skills and experience, but more importantly, it provides valuable insight into the servant's attitude towards work. For example, someone who has repeatedly quit or been fired because "the boss was an asshole" will almost certainly carry this same attitude into their service relationship.

We do want to emphasize that it is uncommon for a normal, well-adjusted adult to require any kind of "obedience" training, provided they genuinely want to serve. In particular, if the servant has been able to consistently hold some kind of paid employment in the outside world, the master can safely assume the servant is *capable* of working to a reasonable standard under the direction of another person, under the right circumstances. If they haven't had much opportunity for paid employment, they can still be evaluated on their ability to take care of themselves and their normal adult responsibilities.

When a servant is capable of doing better in the "real world", but cannot meet reasonable expectations of performance in a power dynamic relationship, generally it is because they see this relationship as a fantasy role or an escape from their ordinary life. If that is what they want out of the relationship, it is essential that they find a master who wants more of a fantasy role, and does not expect the servant to bring their "real world" skills and abilities into the relationship.

If a master is interested, with thorough training, even some of the most escapist servants may be able to provide reliable, competent service in areas that don't remind them at all of their "real world" responsibilities. Others need to have a space to be a brat (or a footstool, or whatever it is they do), but can also shift gears and provide reliable service if given clear boundaries about what is "work" and what is "play".

There are also are s-types who have the desire and capability for a real service relationship, but are acting out behavioral patterns they've learned in past relationships or in childhood. Some are young and inexperienced, some are older and never "grew up". Often they don't understand what the problem is and don't know any other way to act. The right master, with the right style of training, can bring an s-type like this to a place where they flourish in service, but it will not happen without substantial effort from an experienced master. They often benefit from a very structured, controlled training environment, where they initially have an extremely restricted role and gradually earn the privilege of rendering useful service, using their own judgment, and expressing their opinion. With an experienced, skilled master, this type of training program can produce an acceptable servant out of almost anyone who sticks with it. This a remedial obedience program, however, and while it may have recreational value, is generally unnecessary for a responsible, well adjusted, obedient s-type.

On the other hand, some bad behaviors are the result of much deeper issues which cannot be addressed with this type of training. In order to make a distinction between the severity of these types of behavior, we have listed several classic bad s-type behaviors below, divided into two categories. We're calling them "misdemeanors" and "felonies". The misdemeanors can generally be addressed by skillful training, whereas the felonies leave little or no hope of establishing a meaningful service relationship.

The appropriate response to misdemeanors is a serious conversation with the servant about the reasons for their behavior and their commitment to the relationship, and corrective measures must address the underlying problem as well as the behavior. Masters should note that the misdemeanors are signs that there is something fundamentally amiss with the servant's understanding of their role. They should be addressed promptly, regardless of whether the behavior itself is bothersome to the master.

The appropriate response to felonies is for the master to take a hard look at whether the relationship should continue at all. We've spoken to quite a few masters who have tolerated repeated "felony"-type behaviors from unstable s-types because they felt they were partially responsible, because the servant blamed the master for causing the behavior, or because the master felt an obligation to "fix" the servant. Except in very rare circumstances, these are problems that are well beyond the ability of even an extremely good master to solve. If there is a valued long-term relationship with the s-type in question, the best course of action is to focus on the non-service aspects of the relationship, and get them some kind of professional help, if they will accept it.

Misdemeanors

- Not taking the master's orders or corrections seriously.
- Misrepresenting their skills and experience level.
- Continually arguing with orders, apparently for the joy of winning an argument.
- Rules-lawyering (attempting to find loopholes in the master's orders).
- Disobeying in the hope of getting "funishment".
- Disobeying in order to see if the rules still stand.
- Disobeying in order to manipulate the master into giving them a takedown and emotional catharsis.
- Disobeying because they have issues with authority figures in general.
- Disobeying due to poor self-control.
- Picking fights with other members of the household, or attempting to get other s-types in trouble.
- Repeatedly misinterpreting or misremembering orders to their own benefit.
- Creative Applied Incompetence (feigning incompetence at any task they dislike in the hopes of avoiding it in the future).
- Continually avoiding work, or meeting only the bare minimum standards for their performance with no interest in doing better.
- Publicly complaining about the master in order to get sympathy from others, and concealing this behavior from their master.
- Breaking or losing valuable items due to carelessness.
- Stealing, destroying, or intentionally disposing of small items of negligible value.
- Refusing to acknowledge their behavior is problematic.

&ep; Consistent pattern of looking for excuses, repeated preventable mistakes, or a general unwillingness to take responsibility for their own behavior.

Felonies

- Repeated or elaborate lying about any substantial issue.

- Breaking rules regarding their sexual activities with other people.

- Being sexually inappropriate around the master's children or with their belongings.

- Stealing, destroying, or intentionally disposing of valuable items.

- Secretly looking for a new master to replace the one they are currently serving.

- Threats or acts of physical aggression against the master or other members of the household, or uncontrolled displays of anger which result in damage to the master's belongings.

- Drug or alcohol abuse, or uncontrolled mental illness.

- Threatening to report the master to the police for abusive behavior, or expose the master's private life to family members, work, or the public.

Questioning Orders and Disagreeing With Respect

In anything more than the most superficial relationship, the servant will eventually have to come to terms with their master's various flaws and shortcomings. The servant will find areas where their own knowledge and skill exceeds that of the master, and they will occasionally notice things the master has overlooked. The servant will inevitably have strong opinions that differ from their master's, because that's the way it is with any two people who live with one close to the other's business.

In a mature and healthy relationship, the servant is able to offer advice and contrary opinions respectfully, in a manner appropriate to their role and acceptable to their master, without either person feeling that this is a challenge to the master's authority. However, offering opinions and advice is frequently a privilege granted only to experienced and trusted servants, and it is not at all unhealthy for a master to restrict a servant's right to voice their opinion until the servant has earned it.

For an inexperienced and insecure servant, offering advice to the master can put the master in a no-win situation. If the master accepts the advice, the servant may see the master as unsure of themselves, but if the master rejects it, the servant may be upset at having their advice disregarded. If the master accepts the advice and the situation goes badly, the servant may feel like they are responsible for the master's decisions and cannot trust the master to protect them. If the master rejects the advice and it goes badly, the servant is rarely able to resist an "I told you so!" Unfortunately, an inexperienced servant may be equally distressed if prohibited from offering advice, deciding the master is insecure or even abusive. It is a difficult issue, and a master may need to do a good deal of communication in order to make the servant understand and appreciate their reasoning.

Almost all reasonable and sensible masters allow a certain amount of questioning, if only so the servant can make sure that they fully understand the order. Any master who doesn't even allow that had better be giving extremely explicit orders, followed up by a "Do you understand?" That's rare, though, and an awful lot of work for the master. In general, asking for clarification of orders in a reasonably respectful tone of voice will work fine. Where it gets tricky is when the servant feels that the order has serious flaws, and feels the need to point these out to the master in the hopes that they will alter the order. Some masters claim not to care how the question is phrased, but in our experience they all tend to be generally happier when questioning of orders is done in a respectful way. Certainly it cuts down on arguments, in dynamics where arguing is permitted.

One simple way to start is to assume that the master lacks specific information, and to deliver that information as a flat statement. If you are told to take out the trash, saying, "The trash man already came earlier today," and leaving it at that, is more helpful and less challenging than "Don't you know that the trash man already came?" or "You want me to take the trash out and let it sit by the curb for a week?" Phrasing the problem as a statement of information allows the master to integrate it at will, and change orders if necessary.

Another possibility is "May I suggest an alternate solution?" The hard part with this, however, is that the servant must not take it personally or become upset if the master rejects their wonderful solution – or even more difficult, says, "No" to the initial request, and doesn't even want to hear the wonderful solution. It's important that the master feels they have the right to say no to the servant's suggestions. If it's been negotiated that the servant's perspective is considered a valuable tool, or the master is clear that the servant is more skilled than them at something, a wise master will probably listen if only to have the information. However, they are not obligated to do so, and the servant should not be attempting to push that obligation on them, however much they would like it to be so. The master's right to refuse the servant is one of the underpinnings of any power dynamic.

Another way in which this problem can manifest is in asking for help. For some power dynamics, it's acceptable for the servant to ask the master to help with a task if it looks a bit overwhelming. This is especially the case for live-in relationships with a very informal dynamic where people share chores. Ours is one of those, but we quickly ran into trouble with Joshua asking for Raven's help with random jobs. Raven was willing to help if a job was going to fail without aid, and he was sometimes willing to help even if Joshua could handle the job himself but knew it would go faster and more pleasantly with help. However, Raven couldn't always tell which situation it was without further questioning, and in an emergency situation there wasn't time for that. Also, we both agreed that it felt right for us to have the rule that Raven could always say "No" to Joshua if he felt it was appropriate, no matter what the issue. In order to always have the option of saying "No" to non-emergency assistance, in-the-moment phrasing changes were in order. We settled, again, on statements versus questions. A question – "Could you help me with this?" was a non-emergency situation where help might be nice but wasn't necessary. Emergency situations – where the job was going to fail if aid was not quickly rendered – are phrased as statements. "I need your help. That top piece is about to fall off, and I don't have a free hand to grab it."

Voicing emotional discomfort with an order is different from voicing a disagreement with that order, especially in relationships where the servant has explicitly agreed to obey any order that does not cause them serious physical or psychological harm. One M/s couple worked out a series of responses for the s-type to use that worked even in very formal circumstances. If there was no problem with the order, the response was "Yes, sir." In order to communicate "I don't like this order, but I'll do it," the response was, "If it pleases you, sir." In order to communicate "I really don't like this order, and I am registering an objection, but if you don't rescind it I will do it anyway," the response was, "*Only* if it pleases you, sir."

Sometimes it can be difficult for the servant to figure out if the master's mumbled comment is an actual order or simply vague musings. Raven is especially prone to thinking out loud around Joshua, and Joshua is a rather literal person. We've also found that the phrase "Is that an order?" has too many negative connotations from its general use as a term of defiance. It's very hard for most servants to ask that question without sounding somewhat disgruntled, especially if they *are* disgruntled, so instead we instituted the rule that Joshua must answer "Yes, sir," to acknowledge all orders. That policy works well on its own, if only because it means that Raven knows that he heard the order, but it also means that if Joshua misinterprets random musings as an order, Raven can quickly correct him before he attempts to follow through. If "Yes, sir," or "Yes, ma'am," is used throughout the day as a general response, perhaps a more specific version for acknowledging unclear potential orders would be to repeat it back or paraphrase it: "Yes, ma'am. Throw the cat out of the house now before you kill it."

Gender and Service

Talking about gender inevitably involves stereotypes and generalities, cultural biases, and a wide variety of opinions. It is difficult, if not impossible, to say anything definitively about gender roles that will be applicable to everyone in every situation. But regardless of your gender or sexual orientation, it can be useful to look at the ways that gender roles influence your expectations of service.

Some M-types prefer their servants to only provide services that are congruent with the gendered labor assigned to them by "traditional" social roles – for example, only requiring "women's work" of a female servant, and vice-versa. On the other hand, some require services outside of – or even opposed to – those roles. Asking for "gender inappropriate" services can be simply pragmatic – the master just wants the task done – or it can be a deliberate challenge to the servant's gender identity. Upsetting a few of the props holding up a servant's social gender (and their assumptions therein) can be another way in which the M-type redefines the s-type's identity as "whatever I want it to be, not what you've been taught all your life that it should be." It's also another way to show their control – "You'll do the things I tell you to do, not just the ones that make you feel manly or womanly."

Ironically, when we see M-types inflicting this on a s-type, it's the traditionally-feminine female servants who tend to get the most upset. Because accepting the cultural definition of cooking, cleaning, child care, etc. as "women's work" is associated with the assumption of female submission, some female servants have extremely strong emotional attachments to it. They may have eroticized it to a certain extent. They may have conflated their femininity – not just their female gender, but their performance of that gender in a stereotypically feminine way – with their submission itself, and women's work is a badge of both for them. They may have sought out a power dynamic because they idealized the "traditional" housewife role, and they expect that they'll never have to do the kind of labor that represents "independent female doing men's work" again. For them to be forced to do heavy labor, home or car repair, yard work, and especially the chores that require them to get sweaty and filthy often triggers a barrage of complaints and rebellion.

Still, while it's a matter of preference, some M-types have learned that to tell their femme s-types, "Yes, my pretty princess, you are going to learn to change the oil in the car," is a power play that can have surprising results – if the servant doesn't flee in shock. In more all-encompassing power dynamics, this can also be a way of saying, "I own all of you, not just your persona."

Masculine male servants, in contrast, generally expect that they will be made to perform general housework and cleaning regardless of their gender. Because of that association of "women's work" with submission, it's usually the first nonsexual services that an M-type of either gender expects of their servant. This makes it easier for some to think of it as "service work" rather than gendered work, and male servants may not have a problem with it unless it is specifically assigned by a M-type in order to be humiliating.

Yet while they may easily assign their male servants dishes and floor-scrubbing, it may not occur to female masters to have their male servant learn to provide pampering services such as pedicures and massage. Some male submissives, especially of the "sissy maid" type, are very enthusiastic about providing this type of service, but a more conventionally masculine servant may be taken aback by the idea (which may amuse the master, depending on their inclinations). While female masters are often reluctant to assign child care to a male servant, especially if he has no experience being the primary caregiver for children, once a certain level of trust is established, this can be a very valuable service.

In same-sex relationships, the gender of chores may not be nearly as big a deal. Same-sex couples generally have a lot of experience with negotiating chores outside of social roles. Since households generally require the same basic types of chores regardless of the genders of the people living in them and regardless of whether the people involved consider a certain task to be "men's work" or "women's" work, someone is going to wind up doing it. As that would happen anyway, it's easier to make the division in a power dynamic less about gendered work and more about s-type's work versus Master's work (the latter being whatever the M-type decides that they don't want to do).

Some same-sex couples eroticize (usually a somewhat queered version of) traditional heterosexual roles, such as butch/femme lesbianism or the gay male equivalent. If there is a power dynamic present, they face the same issues that M/f and F/m couples do – occasionally with a bit of extra guilt over "giving in" to straight memes, or a certain satisfaction in "subverting" them. If the roles aren't that clear-cut, the couple will have to sift out all the connotations together.

However, if a person doesn't identify with their traditional assigned gender role, for whatever reason, they may be very uncomfortable if they are expected to render services they closely associate with their originally assigned role. An example might be ordering a butch-identified woman to take on a housewife role, or ordering a "sissy maid" cross-dressing man to do car work. For some of them, their service relationship is the only place where their nontraditional gender identity can be fully expressed, respected, or valued. Transsexuals of either direction are harder to classify. Some maintain a knee-jerk dislike of work associated with their original assigned gender for their entire lives, while others transition, settle into their new genders, and become much more comfortable with a wide range of skills and activities not limited to any social gender.

What the master needs to keep in mind is that a servant with a nontraditional gender role may have struggled for much of their life with shame or rejection because of their inability or aversion to performing a socially defined gender role. When they put themselves in a vulnerable position to someone who they hope respects and values them for who they are, being told to do tasks closely associated with that rejected gender role is likely to bring up a lot of difficult emotions. If it is approached mindfully, it can be a real opportunity for growth, but for this to work, the servant usually needs to know that the master deeply understands and respects both their preferred gender role and their struggle with their originally assigned role. While a strong identification with traditional gender roles is frequently just habitual, non-traditional gender roles are much more likely to be seen as essential to the core self.

For a servant with a traditional gender role, work that challenges that role often offers the servant a previously unexplored area. It might be scary, and it might be hard to adjust to, but it is usually new ground for the servant. Challenging a non-traditional gender role, on the other hand, likely brings the servant back to a familiar battleground, confronting painful issues they have struggled with for much of their life. This isn't to say it can't be done, or that it ought not to be done, but it should be approached with caution.

Qualities of a Good Master

Joshua wrote this list for someone who wished to be a master and wanted to know what qualities to cultivate, but it serves equally well as qualities for a submissive to look for when seeking a master. Being a good master is more than just being a good person; it is being a good person when in control of someone else.

Obviously, different people hold different standards, but here are some qualities Joshua personally would expect of a good master. These are in no particular order, with the genders arbitrarily alternated throughout:

- He has impeccable honor. He has a clearly defined moral code and he actually lives by it. While he needn't be completely perfect, he needs to be significantly better than most people in this, in order to be trusted with complete control over another person. He is well aware of any areas where he has difficulty holding consistently to his moral code, and he is always working to improve. He recognizes quickly when he has acted dishonorably, and seeks to make amends in whatever way he can.

- She can clearly state her core values and priorities, and her words and actions reflect them. When her priorities are unflattering, she is honest with herself about them, even if she chooses to keep them private.

- His philosophical and/or spiritual beliefs, especially with regard to honor, responsibility, leadership, and service, are sincerely held and not merely self-serving. He has some concept of something greater than his personal will or ego, if only the common good of society.

- She acts honorably when she has "real world" power over someone, such as her children, pets, or employees. She treats service personnel with courtesy, and is comfortable receiving personal service. She is not derisive towards or made uncomfortable by people of a lower social station.

- He acts honorably when someone has "real world" power over him. Even if he dislikes acting under anyone else's direction, it does not make him irrational or petty. He acts politely and reasonably to his boss, police officers, judges, and the like. He is not derisive towards or made uncomfortable by people of a higher social station.

- She knows her limitations and failings, and can respond maturely to someone pointing them out, even when they do so rudely. She genuinely appreciates constructive criticism from an appropriate source, even when it is difficult for her to hear.

- He knows what he wants and makes no apologies for it. He knows the difference between what he wants and what he can have, and handles such disappointments with maturity. He does not feel excessive guilt or discomfort about desiring control over another person, and feels he can act on these feelings without violating his ethical or spiritual beliefs.

- She knows clearly the difference between fantasy and reality, and can function in reality. She knows the difference between truth and fiction, and is honest unless she has good reason not to be. She knows the difference between telling lies, being honestly mistaken, and being willfully ignorant, both in reference to her own statements and those of others. She operates under a fairly internally consistent logic that is in harmony with her perception of reality. She is not actively mentally ill in any significant way.

- He has no addictions, obsessions, or compulsions that seriously interfere with his ability to make decisions.

- She takes responsibility for her words and actions. In crisis, she doesn't look first for someone or something to blame. She understands and accepts the consequences of her actions, both long and short term.

- He understands that the best plans fail occasionally, even when every possible effort has been made, and that no one is perfect. He can do honest risk assessment and make back-up plans, and cope with failures maturely and constructively.

&ϖ She has her life in good order, for the most part, and does not live crisis to crisis. She does not seem to invite turmoil into her life without good reason.

&ϖ He is reliable. If he says he will do something, you can trust that he will make every effort to do it. If he knows there is a significantly higher than normal chance of failure in a plan, he strives to make this clear beforehand to the parties concerned.

&ϖ Her judgment is sound. She makes better choices than most in tough situations, and is not paralyzed by difficult or unpleasant choices. She has good reasons for her decisions, regardless of whether she explains them to others.

&ϖ He understands his emotions and copes with them reasonably well. He has someone in his life with whom he can express his emotions, if only a therapist or clergyperson.

&ϖ She controls her temper flawlessly. She does not act on sadistic urges (emotional or physical) in inappropriate ways, even under stress. She does not respond violently without serious physical provocation.

Qualities of a Good Servant

After writing the last article, we wanted to create a matching one for the opposite number. It seems that there aren't a lot of standards for what it means to be a good s-type; in fact, there is a distressing tendency for people to casually assume that "of course submissives can't be expected to act like a reliable, committed, self-disciplined adult – they're submissives, aren't they?" This kind of infantilizing of all s-types is counterproductive, as it hardly encourages them to excellence, and indeed it does the opposite. It may stem from a general discomfort with the state of submission on both sides of the slash, where that discomfort is translated into pretending that servants are a lesser class of human. Instead of this, it would be better to see this position as an honorable one – and that means having standards. So here are some ideal characteristics for people in service. (Again, genders are arbitrarily alternated.)

- She is genuinely moved to service because of the emotional happiness it gives her, not because she feels that it is required for a particular fantasy role. She is aware of the difference between fantasy service and reality.

- He honestly enjoys working under the direction of someone else, and rarely suffers from reflexive resentment from being told what to do. He's not exceptionally attached to doing things his own way.

- She enjoys helping people and being useful, but doesn't take it personally if someone refuses her help or doesn't find her service beneficial.

- He takes pride in his work, and is motivated to do a good job without needing praise or recognition.

- While she is able to relax and take time for herself, in general she'd rather be working than sitting around doing nothing.

❧ He isn't a martyr. While he might be quicker than some people to inconvenience himself for the benefit of others, he doesn't go out of his way to inflict hardships on himself for little discernible benefit. He never intentionally makes other people feel guilty over the service he has rendered them or hardships he has endured on their behalf.

❧ She does not need to be sexually aroused to render quality service, and sex is not her main motivation for doing it.

❧ He does not have trust issues so huge that even an extremely honorable master will be under constant paranoid scrutiny for the inevitable betrayal. He is able to realistically assess whether the judgment of a given master is worth trusting, and can relax into being carried by their will.

❧ She has a sense of honor and will strive to do the right thing even when it is unpleasant. She obeys not because she is afraid of consequences, but because she has made a commitment to do so. She takes pride in being able to remain obedient even when it is extremely difficult for her.

❧ He is reliable. If he says he will do something, you can trust that he will make every effort to do it. Keeping his commitments is very important to him.

❧ She has reasonably good self-control, and does not require continual external management of her volatile emotions. She is not actively mentally ill.

❧ He has no addictions, obsessions, or compulsions that seriously interfere with his ability to follow orders.

❧ She is capable of acting with discretion when allowed access to confidential or sensitive personal information. She is not inclined to gossip, and can keep secrets without drama.

❧ He can clearly and respectfully communicate any difficulties, concerns, or potential conflicts regarding his orders, in a manner appropriate to his role. He does not take it personally if the master rejects his suggestions.

❧ She is willing to admit when she does not understand something, or doesn't think she is capable of it. She is willing to fully apply herself to a task, even if she thinks it is beyond her capabilities.

- He is not looking for a service relationship in order to avoid real-world responsibility or accountability. He sees himself as a mature and responsible adult, capable of making good decisions.

- She realistically evaluates how the other responsibilities and commitments in her life effect how much service she is able to offer and under what circumstances, and clearly communicates this to the people she serves.

- He understands what he is hoping to get out of a service relationship. He can clearly communicate what he expects in return for his service, and what he would like but is willing to compromise on. If he is not getting these things, he discusses it with his master in a timely manner, rather than silently building up resentment.

- She accepts that her master is a real and imperfect human being. She does not hold unrealistic ideas about her master's perfection, but is not excessively critical of her master's flaws.

- He's comfortable working "behind the scenes" and isn't particularly concerned with whether his contributions are publically acknowledged.

- She finds service to be an honorable and fulfilling way of life that makes good use of her skills. She does not feel it is a waste of her time, or that the work is "beneath her".

- He is able to appreciate that different people have different values and priorities, and can act according to his master's priorities, even when they differ substantially from his own.

- She is genuinely comfortable with her place in the household hierarchy. She does not look for ways to feel superior to other servants or to the people she serves. She does not attempt to look good at the expense of others.

- He is has good observational skills, and can figure out his master's habits, preferences, and priorities over time.

- She is able to understand her master's view of life well enough to be able to extrapolate what her master would want her to do in any given situation, and follow those unwritten orders in a manner appropriate to her position.

- He has a good sense of his own worth as a person and as a servant, and will not serve a master who does not value him. He knows that he cannot honorably serve a dishonorable person.

- She can realistically assess her skill level, experience level, and how her physical and mental condition at any time will affect her job performance. She knows how to communicate this information clearly to her master in a way that is useful to them.

- He is able to understand his master's relationships with other people – such as other servants, submissives, slaves, egalitarian partners, family, and friends – and values them because they make his master happy in some way.

- She is able to verbally defend her chosen lifestyle to questioners, where appropriate, in terms that express how good the power dynamic is for her self-esteem and overall welfare.

Skillsets

Service Skills

The skill lists that follow are meant to give ideas and examples to masters and servants and to get them talking about service in terms of "real world" activities. They are also provided to give masters inspiration as to how their servants could provide useful service. We hope these lists will also provide servants with ideas about skills they might like to learn, as well as prompt them to offer skills they already have but never thought to offer in their power-dynamic relationship. The selection and categorization of skills is based on our way of life and experiences, and the daily lives of the other people we know in service. Like any lists of this sort, it reflects our personal biases, values, and preferences.

Skills are categorized into three levels:

Remedial skills are skills we think it is reasonable to assume that any competent adult be able to do.

Basic skills are what we'd expect to be within the capabilities of most servants who routinely provide service in an area.

Advanced skills are specialized skills that someone focusing on that area of service would not necessarily be *expected* to have, but that a servant with more experience might be able to offer. Many require a strong aptitude for the task, specific training, or fairly extensive

Please Note: It is entirely possible that an otherwise competent adult may, for whatever reason, have very limited exposure to a certain area of service, so I don't mean to imply that anyone who lacks these *remedial skills* is stupid or was raised by wolves.

However, if a servant lacks any of the *remedial skills* in a given area, and is asked to provide any service at all in that area, they are advised to clearly and promptly explain their lack of experience to their master, even if the requested service itself seems clear. This way, the master will be able to assess the servant's knowledge and skills more thoroughly, and provide the necessary supervision and instruction.

study.

There are some terms which we use in a precise way in this section, and they also describe three very different ways of rendering service. These terms will be italicized in the skills lists in order to show that this precise definition is intended.

❧ *Detailed instructions* make very few, if any, assumption about the servant's prior knowledge. They do not require the servant make any complex decisions with regard to implementing them. They are specific enough that it would be exceedingly difficult to do the task badly while accurately following the instructions. The master knows exactly how to do the task, and barring physical limitations, is able to do the task themselves. The master takes responsibility for verifying that the servant knows exactly what to do, and has thought about where the servant might need more clarification due to limited knowledge or experience.

❧ *Basic instructions* assume that the servant has the essential skills required for the task, and if they haven't done this exact task before, they are familiar enough with similar tasks that they are confident that they can achieve the specified result. The master might not know exactly how to do the task, but has a general idea. While the master generally has a specific result in mind, the servant may need to make reasonable assumptions about some of the details. The servant is expected to ask questions to clarify ambiguity or complications the master hasn't thought of, but overall, the master takes responsibility for ensuring that what they asked for will produce a desirable outcome.

❧ *Minimal instruction* assumes that the servant is very familiar with all aspects of the service. The servant is expected to make complex decisions with regard to methods used, and generally is given a great deal of flexibility with regard to the specific tasks. The master may have little or no understanding of what is involved in performing the service. The master may only have a very general idea about what they want, so experience and good judgment are required to assure an acceptable result. The servant asks few, if any, questions of the master about details of the tasks, and only occasional questions about the overall goal. If the master requests things without understanding the repercussions of the order, it is the servant's responsibility to inform them of this in an appropriate way. The servant is responsible for ensuring the outcome is desirable to the master.

For example, if the master has a flower garden that the servant works on, *detailed instructions* would include exactly what work was to be done today, exactly what supplies to buy, what planting, weeding, and watering to do today, etc. *Basic instructions* might specify the type of plants and the area to be planted, and what time of year certain tasks need to be accomplished, but the servant would need to figure out exactly what to buy, how to put it in, and figure out a reasonable daily maintenance schedule. *Minimal instructions* might include only the occasional comment about wanting "something more colorful" in a specified area, or "more shrubs", or "something fancy like we saw at Susan's."

Without prompting means that once it is established that this service is the servant's responsibility, they are expected to do it as needed, with no further orders or reminders. For routine tasks, this may mean doing it according to a set schedule, or independently coming up with a schedule that produces a satisfactory result. Some tasks may need to be done only a few times a year, but to do them *without prompting* still means that no reminder from the master is needed or expected. The servant is certainly free to arrange for their own "prompting", such as reminders on a calendar. The system by which they remember to do things is irrelevant, so long as it is effective. Do not underestimate what a valuable service it is to relieve someone of the responsibility of keeping track of something. However, both master and servant should be careful of any miscommunication about whose responsibility it is to keep track of a given thing.

One further note: When we specify something being done in a "reasonable" manner or by a "reasonable" method, we mean doing it in a way that suits the needs of an average person. This is only specified for skills where a significantly more advanced level of competency is possible and in some cases desirable, but many reasonable people do not consider it mandatory when performing the task for themselves. For instance, a person can do laundry in a *reasonable manner* if they can get their own moderately soiled clothes clean without damaging them, and put them away in drawers or on hangers. It is not reasonable to assume an average person knows how to launder items that they themselves do not wear, just as it is not reasonable to assume that an average person would automatically read every clothing tag, hand-wash undergarments, use certain laundry additives, fold items crisply and uniformly, or put clothing away sorted by a particular system. If a master wants things done according a certain way, they should be make that clear.

Occasionally, due to vastly different upbringings, a master and servant have wildly different ideas about what constitutes a reasonable method. In our experience this is rare, and the overwhelming majority of "misunderstandings" with regard to what constitutes a reasonable method are due to the servant's passive-aggressive behavior, mental illness, or substance abuse. Certainly the second such "misunderstanding", if not the first, should be met with a direct and firm confrontation.

If the servant believes it is the master who is making unreasonable assumptions, the servant should respectfully initiate a direct conversation about the issue. While such misunderstandings may be due to ignorance of the servant's experience, they often indicate the master has made little effort to make their expectations clear or to assess the capabilities of the servant. Sometimes this comes from an unspoken desire to punish or berate the servant, or a misguided attempt at "training", both of which suggest a relationship dynamic that many service-oriented submissives will find they are unsuited for.

Fundamental Service Skills

Remedial Skills:

ॐ Show up on time.

ॐ Obey instructions under direct supervision.

ॐ Ask for clarification of orders if they are unclear to you.

ॐ Take constructive criticism without emotional outbursts.

ॐ Be present with someone, without interfering with what they are doing or requiring constant attention.

ॐ Honestly report your mistakes and errors in a timely manner.

ॐ Remain silent when told to shut up.

Basic Skills:

ॐ Obey instructions without supervision.

ॐ Assess whether or not your performance meets a specified standard.

ॐ Adjust your performance of a given task based on time and resources available.

ॐ Estimate time required to reasonably accomplish multiple tasks.

ॐ Gracefully handle interruption of your work.

ॐ Adjust to changes in your routine.

ॐ Concentrate on a task despite distractions.

ॐ Use reasonable problem-solving skills.

ॐ Complete routine tasks on a specified schedule, with *basic instructions*.

ॐ Remember a list of tasks, writing it down if needed, *without prompting*.

ॐ Research and learn a simple unfamiliar task with *minimal instruction*.

ॐ Assess when literal interpretation of an order is not appropriate due to unforeseen circumstances.

- Offer a concise and accurate summary of events, without opinions, suggestions, commentary, or excessive bias.
- Create and implement a backup plan for foreseeable failures.
- Respectfully express a contradictory point of view.
- Respectfully bring potential problems or oversights to the master's attention.
- Accept criticism gracefully, in private and in public.
- Maintain your own health and emotional well-being, *with minimal instruction*, asking for assistance when appropriate.

Advanced Skills:

- Anticipatory service – know enough about your master's preferences to make accurate assumptions about services they might want, but have not yet asked for.
- Supervise other servants, in accordance with specified rules of behavior.
- Train other servants in specific tasks and skills.
- Coordinate complex tasks involving multiple people.
- Find and hire paid professionals.
- Independently develop and implement a plan to achieve a complex goal specified by the master.
- Independently add useful skills to your repertoire.

Housework

Remedial Skills:

- ◈ Remove trash, dirty laundry, and dirty dishes from a living space without unnecessarily disturbing other items.
- ◈ Clean specified surfaces when provided with appropriate tools and products, and *basic instructions.*
- ◈ Put items where they belong, when given *basic instructions.*
- ◈ Clean up spills in a reasonable manner, *without prompting.*
- ◈ Empty wastebaskets and replace trash bags, *without prompting.*
- ◈ Sort items into easily identifiable, unambiguous categories.
- ◈ Vacuum and sweep the floor.
- ◈ Wash dishes by hand and use a dishwasher in a reasonable manner.

Basic Skills:

- ◈ Select appropriate tools and cleaning products for different surfaces and use them appropriately.
- ◈ Return specified items to where they belong, on an ongoing basis, *without prompting.*
- ◈ Keep specified floors and surfaces clean on an ongoing basis, *without prompting.*
- ◈ Keep dishes washed and put away on an ongoing basis, *without prompting.*
- ◈ Put away items in a moderately organized living space, making

> Following the example of Jack McGeorge, we think of "clean" and "tidy" as two distinct concepts. Cleaning is removing dirt, washing surfaces, dusting, etc. Tidying is putting things where they belong and ensuring everything is in order. It is entirely possible to do one without the other. If there is limited time available, tidying a space frequently improves its usability more than cleaning. Alternately, if the servant doesn't know where things go, or the master prefers to keep things lying around, the servant can clean without tidying.

reasonable assumptions about where items go, with *minimal instruction.*

𐁯 Organize a specified area, given *basic instructions.*

𐁯 Keep the entire interior of the home clean and tidy on an ongoing basis, according to *basic instructions.*

Advanced Skills:

𐁯 Keep the interior of the home clean and tidy on an ongoing basis, *without prompting.*

𐁯 Organize specified areas with *minimal instruction.*

𐁯 Care for furniture, dishes, and surfaces which require special treatment.

A Note On Keeping House

While some masters insist on a house being kept according to a very strict standard, in many power-dynamic relationships, the servant is far more concerned with the cleanliness of the house than the master. For whatever reason, some masters put a very low priority on housework, and prefer to allocate their servant's time elsewhere. This is often the case with Raven, and when Joshua has talked to other servants in a similar position, all have struggled with feeling like a failure for not keeping the house "clean enough". Often there is a surprising amount of shame about what other people will think of the servant, or what the servant's mother would say about it. Please refer to the First Rule of Service, and know that you have Joshua's sympathy, at least. Masters in this position should not give in to any pressure the servant attempts to exert regarding the issue, as it sets a very bad precedent. After the priorities have been firmly established, the master might consider allowing the servant to clean the house in their "free time". Raven generally considers cleaning to be a "hobby" of Joshua's, not a service.

That said, Joshua recommend two books to servants passionate about housekeeping, or hesitantly approaching housekeeping for the first time. The first is *Home Comforts: The Art and Science of Keeping House* by Cheryl Mendelson. Not only is this a very comprehensive reference, Mendelson's attitude towards housekeeping is delightful. If nothing else, the introduction provides a wonderful example of someone who approaches housekeeping as an enjoyable and rewarding activity, not some dreaded obligation to be finished as quickly as possible. She provides a great deal of information for the absolute beginner, but also detailed reference information and advanced techniques appropriate for more experienced folks.

It is a wonderful book for the detail-oriented servant whose master has provided ample time for housekeeping, but distressingly little detail about how the house should be kept. If a servant would really like diagrams to show the proper method for folding underpants, this is the book to get. It is essential however, that the servant not become so invested in doing things "by the book" that they disregard the master's preferences.

Joshua's second recommendation is *Keeping House: The Litany of Everyday Life* by Margaret Kim Peterson. Peterson is a Christian who finds the virtues of hospitality and service beautifully embodied in the daily work of feeding, clothing, and otherwise caring for a family and home. This book does not contain housekeeping techniques, but is a passionately and thoughtfully written personal exploration of housekeeping as a spiritual path.

Home Maintenance

Remedial Skills:

- Change light bulbs.
- Paint fences or walls where precision is not required, when given *detailed instructions*.
- Use a screwdriver and hammer in a safe and reasonable manner.

Basic Skills:

- Unclog a drain or toilet.
- Replace or repair sink fixture, showerhead, toilet tank parts, accessible leaky pipe, light fixture.
- Install common large appliances (washing machine, dryer, dishwasher, stove, etc.)
- Paint interior walls and hang wallpaper, with *minimal instruction*.
- Fix squeaky hinges, doors that don't latch, drawers that stick, etc., with *minimal instruction*.
- Assemble furniture from a kit and put up shelving.
- Hang a picture.
- Consistently drive a nail straight.
- Have a well-stocked toolbox.
- Use common power tools (circular saw, electric sander, power drill) confidently.
- Patch drywall.
- Clean gutters.
- Clean the exterior of a house.

Advanced Skills:

- Install a toilet, sink, or tub.
- Basic carpentry and furniture repair.

- Basic construction, drywall, framing, roofing, concrete, etc.
- Basics of home electrical wiring and plumbing.
- Paint exterior of home.
- Install and refinish flooring.
- Do all needed minor maintenance and repairs on an ongoing basis, *without prompting*.
- Evaluate the need for major maintenance and repairs on an ongoing basis, *without prompting*.
- Find and hire professionals to handle major maintenance and repairs, with *minimal instruction*.

Yardwork

Remedial Skills:

- Rake leaves, shovel snow, remove debris, and water plants with *basic instructions*.

Basic Skills:

- Trim bushes, clean gutters, lay sod, spread grass seed or fertilizer, mow lawn, and spread mulch, when given *basic instructions*.
- Weed garden and harvest vegetables, when given *basic instructions*.
- Plant small trees, shrubs, plants and seeds, when given *basic instructions*.
- Keep lawn mowed, leaves raked, snow shoveled, etc. on an ongoing basis *without prompting*.
- Use a gas powered tiller and string trimmer. Drive a ride-on lawnmower or garden tractor.

Advanced Skills:

- Plant, maintain and harvest garden on an ongoing basis, with *minimal instruction*.
- Maintain lawn on an ongoing basis, with *minimal instruction*.
- Use a chainsaw and a hand saw. Remove dangerous limbs from trees. Split firewood.
- Simple landscaping, including small walls and walkways.
- Prune trees, hedges, vines and roses correctly.

Laundry

Remedial Skills:

- Wash and dry your own clothing without damage.
- Fold, hang, and put away clothing in a *reasonable manner*.

Basic Skills:

- Separate clothes by color and wash at the appropriate temperature.
- Make reasonable assumptions about what items are not machine washable.
- Follow care instructions on clothing labels, like "dry flat" or "warm iron only".
- Hang laundry on a line securely and neatly.
- Iron basic clothing items (shirts, pants, straight skirts) at the appropriate temperature, without damaging them.
- Neatly and uniformly fold clothing and linens, including awkward items like fitted sheets.
- Hand-wash delicate items, such as lingerie.
- Sew on lost buttons and make minor repairs.
- Understand the dry-cleaning process, and know a good dry-cleaner in your area.

Advanced Skills:

- Remove difficult stains and use appropriate laundry additives.
- Iron complex clothing, and use starch/sizing appropriately.
- Clean items that require specialized techniques.
- Mend and hem most types of clothing.

Cooking

Remedial Skills:

- ๛ Prepare packaged food according to the instructions on the package.
- ๛ Understand nutritional information and ingredients lists on packaged foods.
- ๛ Make toast, boil pasta, cook an egg, assemble a sandwich, and make coffee and tea reasonably well.
- ๛ Buy and serve take-out food, with non-disposable plates and flatware.
- ๛ Use common kitchen appliances: microwave, toaster, coffee maker, blender, mixer, food processor, dishwasher.
- ๛ Without fear of injury, cook on a gas or electric stove, chop vegetables, grate cheese, and remove hot items from the oven at a specified time.
- ๛ Set a table for an informal dinner, in a *reasonable manner*.
- ๛ Load a dishwasher and wash dishes by hand, in a *reasonable manner*.

Basic Skills:

- ๛ Prepare at least ten different meals suitable for everyday dinner.
- ๛ Prepare a few different fancy meals, for special occasions.
- ๛ Make a few different desserts, including pie and cake.
- ๛ Confidently cook new foods using a recipe.
- ๛ Open wine and beer bottles that don't have screw-tops.
- ๛ Debone raw chicken; carve turkey and large cuts of meat.
- ๛ Understand safe food handling procedures.
- ๛ Shop for groceries on an ongoing basis, given *basic instructions*.
- ๛ Attractively arrange food on a plate.

- ❧ Set a table attractively for a special occasion, not necessarily formal.
- ❧ Serve plates and pour beverages gracefully.
- ❧ Prepare a reasonable meal in a poorly stocked and equipped kitchen.

Advanced Skills:

- ❧ Prepare meals daily, *without prompting.*
- ❧ Cook for 30 or more people.
- ❧ Prepare elaborate multi-course dinners.
- ❧ Bake bread.
- ❧ Thorough knowledge of different wines, beers, and liquors, including what goes with what, and how to prepare several mixed drinks.
- ❧ Thorough knowledge of a specific regional cuisine.
- ❧ Specialized diets: vegetarian, vegan, diabetic, celiac, allergies, etc.
- ❧ Canning, drying, and other food preservation.
- ❧ Cook comfort foods just like the master's mother/grandmother.

Shopping and Errands

Remedial Skills:

- ৯ Stand in line to pay for items.
- ৯ Resist impulse buys.
- ৯ Estimate purchase totals and make change.
- ৯ Buy groceries and other household purchases given *detailed instructions*.
- ৯ Know good stores for clothing of your gender, appropriate to your social group and budget.

Basic Skills:

- ৯ Know good stores in your master's area for a variety of basic products.
- ৯ Understand price-per-unit-costs and be able to compare the prices of differently sized products.
- ৯ Save receipts and keep track of expenditures.
- ৯ Interact effectively with store personnel in order to find items, make special requests, or resolve problems.
- ৯ Find consumer research about available brands and styles of a given product.
- ৯ Keep certain items stocked on an ongoing basis.
- ৯ Find and organize coupons, locate sales, and other bargain-hunting strategies.
- ৯ Shop for and compare products online.
- ৯ Find specialty stores for products you are not familiar with.
- ৯ Know good stores for clothing of the other gender, appropriate to your social group, and be reasonably comfortable shopping there alone.
- ৯ Understand how women's, men's, and children's clothing and shoes are sized.

- Select appropriate gifts and cards for a variety of people and occasions.

- Make reasonable decisions about substitutions for a product that is unavailable.

Advanced Skills:

- Shop for specialty items, such as stock for a business.

- Shop in areas where foreign language usage is necessary.

- Haggle or negotiate for the best price, where appropriate.

Automotive

Remedial Skills:

- Have a driver's license, and be able to drive reasonably safely.
- Drive in an unfamiliar area, when given *detailed instructions.*
- Refuel the car as needed, *without prompting.*
- Have a general idea about what sort of routine maintenance a car needs, and where to go to get these services.
- Understand the local legal requirements for having a car registered, inspected, and insured.

Basic Skills:

- Drive safely *without prompting*, obeying all relevant traffic laws, including speed limit.
- Parallel park confidently.
- Drive a manual transmission.
- Modify driving to account for road condition, low visibility, weather, etc.
- Responsibly and accurately assess your ability to drive when overtired, emotionally distressed, or under the influence of any mind-altering substance (including prescription and non-prescription medication).
- While driving, be aware of any warning lights, unusual sounds, or change in handling of the vehicle, and respond appropriately.
- Resolve common driving emergencies (flat tire, minor accident, car won't start) without assistance from your master.
- Change the oil, check fluids, replace wiper blades, check tire pressure, and change a flat tire.
- Do simple automotive repairs when given proper tools and *detailed instructions.*

Advanced Skills:

- ❧ Handle all aspects of driving and automobile maintenance on an ongoing basis, with *minimal instruction*.

- ❧ Do common automotive repairs yourself, and know reliable professionals to go to for more complex repairs.

- ❧ Confidently drive and navigate in a difficult city, on difficult terrain, or under exceptionally challenging conditions.

- ❧ Safely exceed the speed limit or violate minor traffic regulations, under orders, when appropriate.

Travel

Remedial Skills:

- Pack your own clothing and personal items for a weekend trip, *in a reasonable manner*.
- Check in at an airport and board a plane, given *basic instructions*.
- Understand a bus or train schedule. Travel using the subway or other public transportation in a city you live in or visit often.

Basic Skills:

- Find shops, services, and lodging in a strange location.
- Make reservations for lodging, meals and events.
- Pack someone else's clothing and personal items given *basic instructions*.
- Make reservations for airline travel, taking into account travel times, layovers, airline amenities, and price.
- Understand current restrictions on checked and carry-on baggage.
- Estimate travel time required for a given trip, taking into account traffic, weather, airline rules, etc.
- Compare available travel options (plane, rail, bus, cab, etc) for time, cost, and convenience.
- Travel using public transportation in an unfamiliar city.
- Research tourist attractions and other entertainment at a given destination.
- Plan route for a car trip, including food and rest stops, and estimate time and fuel required.
- Using whatever resources are at your disposal, locate a certain type of store or restaurant in an unfamiliar area.
- Navigate using both a map or a GPS navigation device.

❧ If traveling to a foreign country, learn a few basic phrases in their local languages, and have a phrasebook handy.

Advanced Skills:

❧ Handle all necessary arrangements for domestic travel.

❧ Plan a trip to a foreign country, including currency exchange, passport issues, location of local embassy, important customs, local transportation, applicable laws, and local guide/interpreter if needed.

❧ If traveling in a foreign country, obtain basic proficiency in the language.

Secretarial

Remedial Skills:

❧ Answer the telephone politely, and take an accurate and detailed message.

❧ Keep track of occasional appointments on a calendar or schedule book.

Basic Skills:

❧ Answer the telephone and make calls in a consistently professional manner.

❧ Arrange and schedule meetings and appointments.

❧ Dress and behave appropriately in a business situation.

❧ File papers according to an established system, when given *basic instructions*.

❧ Create a simple filing system for home or small business.

❧ Set up, use and maintain common office technology (fax machine, copier)

❧ Type at least 45 words per minute.

❧ Use a computer for email, word processing, and spreadsheet software.

Advanced Skills:

❧ Provide full secretarial service in a professional office environment.

❧ Manage up to five employees or contract labor.

❧ Type at least 60 words per minute.

Computer/Electronic

Remedial Skills:

- Be able to use a computer for basic tasks: web browsing, email, etc.
- Set a digital clock.
- Operate common household electronics (TV, CD/DVD player, remote controls, etc.), *in a reasonable manner.*

Basic Skills:

- Set up TV, DVD player, video game systems, and similar equipment.
- Back up computer files.
- Set up a simple website.
- Resolve simple problems with computers or electronics, with the help of tech support or other resources.
- Confidently use complex websites (online banking, etc.)

Advanced Skills:

- Resolve most problems with computers or electronics.
- Professional quality web design.
- Computer programming and engineering.

Financial

Remedial Skills:

- Keep your own finances in order, *in a reasonable manner.*
- Keep your spending within a specified budget.

Basic Skills:

- Make a budget to meet specified goals.
- File personal income taxes.
- Balance a checkbook.
- Check bank account balance online.
- Understand interest on mortgages, loans, credit cards, and savings accounts.
- Know what service personnel are customarily tipped, and how much is appropriate.

Advanced Skills:

- Do accounting and keep books for a small business.
- File income taxes for someone who is self-employed, working as an independent contractor, or runs small business.
- Have a thorough knowledge of investment options, retirement plans, etc.

Health Care

Remedial Skills:

- Care for yourself and your own health *in a reasonable manner.*
- Take prescribed medications as directed.
- Have a doctor or health care provider.
- Assess how an illness or injury may affect your ability to do certain tasks.

Basic Skills:

- Learn basic first aid and CPR.
- Be able to accurately fill a med-minder or daily pill dispenser.
- Assist someone with an injury or disability in activities of daily life.
- Use a thermometer, blood pressure cuff, and blood sugar monitor.
- Bandage a moderately severe wound.
- Assess whether an injury is within your ability to treat, or whether professional care is necessary.
- Understand the uses and side effects of your master's prescription medications and your own.
- Safely and courteously push a wheelchair.
- Understand disease transmission, and how to protect yourself and others from communicable diseases (including how to protect yourself from other people's bodily fluids while caring for them), and how to safely interact with immunocompromised people.

Advanced Skills:

- Give health care treatments in a way that feels like a luxury service.

- Perform advanced "in the field" first aid such as suturing wounds, setting broken bones, etc. in an emergency when help is not available.
- Administer injectable medications.
- Medicinal herbalism.
- Personal Care Attendant or Home Health Aide training.
- Caretaking skills for people with serious illness or disability.
- Massage or bodywork certification
- EMT training or other medical certification/degree.

Child Care

Remedial Skills:

- Refrain from sexually inappropriate behavior or obscene language around children.
- Keep reasonably well-behaved children from harm for up to one hour.
- Be able to control your emotional responses when children's behavior distresses or annoys you.

Basic Skills:

- Feed and change a baby.
- Bathe, dress, and feed children.
- Prepare age-appropriate meals.
- Entertain and supervise children for up to six hours.
- Get children ready for school in the morning.
- Assist children with schoolwork.
- Resolve conflicts between children, and calm a distressed child.
- Enforce the rules of the parent/guardian even when you do not agree with them.
- Handle minor first aid and health care (medications, scrapes and bruises, etc.)

Advanced Skills:

- Handle all aspects of childcare on an ongoing basis.
- Have a thorough understanding of childhood development.
- Know how to handle children with special needs, including physical disability, chronic illness, developmental delay, or emotional problems.
- Homeschool and tutor school-age children.

Animal Care

Remedial Skills:

- Care for and clean up after your own pets in a reasonable manner.
- Feed and water common pets (dogs, cats, fish, small caged animals) when given *basic instructions.*

Basic Skills:

- Supervise and clean up after dogs and cats with *minimal instruction.*
- Walk one to three dogs safely.
- Exercise or play with cooperative pets, *in a reasonable manner.*
- Do basic grooming and bathing of cats and dogs.
- Provide routine health care (medications, flea treatments, etc.), *with basic instructions.*
- Clean a fish tank.
- Provide complete care for common pets on an ongoing basis *without prompting,* and for exotic pets and livestock for periods of time, *with basic instructions.*

Advanced Skills:

- Monitor the health of pets and livestock on an ongoing basis.
- Train a reasonably cooperative dog in basic obedience.
- Rehabilitate animals with behavioral problems.

Arts and Crafts

Remedial Skills:

- ❧ Cut and glue paper or cloth in a reasonable manner with *detailed instructions.*
- ❧ Paint simple objects in solid colors.
- ❧ Assist children with simple craft projects.

Basic Skills:

- ❧ Operate a sewing machine. Sew simple clothing or craft projects using a pattern and *detailed instructions.*
- ❧ Knitting or crocheting simple projects.
- ❧ Simple embroidery and appliqué.
- ❧ Decorative painting and stenciling.
- ❧ Scrapbooking.
- ❧ Simple woodworking with hand and small power tools.
- ❧ Assembling wood projects from a kit.
- ❧ Simple live flower arrangements, and attractive use of silk flowers.

Advanced Skills:

- ❧ Tailoring clothing for men and women.
- ❧ Constructing custom clothing without patterns.
- ❧ Constructing elaborate costumes.
- ❧ Knitting/crocheting shaped clothing and complex patterns.
- ❧ Elaborate embroidery and appliqué.
- ❧ Making stained glass.
- ❧ Repairing and reupholstering furniture.
- ❧ Artistic painting (landscapes, portraits, etc.)
- ❧ Cabinetry, furniture-making, and advanced woodworking.
- ❧ Professional-quality floristry.

Companionship

Remedial Skills:

- Hold a conversation that is of interest to the other person.
- Behave appropriately when accompanying someone in public.
- Listen to your master speak without continual interruptions.

Basic Skills:

- Find something enjoyable in participating in any hobby activity with your master.
- Be familiar with the hobbies and pastimes common in your social group, including those of your preferred gender.
- Learn new hobby skills that would please your master, so long as they do not require specialized talents.
- Observe people's physical/voice cues and discern their emotional state with reasonable accuracy in most cases.
- Discern your master's emotional states and figure out what demeanor and tone is appropriate to each one.
- Entertain yourself when you are not actively needed to interact with your master, but required to stay in the general vicinity just in case.
- Be patient, quiet, and unobtrusive when you are "in waiting" – in your master's presence but without interactions with them or current activity assignments.
- Entertain a small group of people at home.
- Be comfortable slow dancing in public.
- Be reasonably charming to anyone in public.
- Come up with interesting conversation topics on the spur of the moment.
- Make your dynamic look "normal" in public – e.g. handle yourself in a way that does not call attention to your dynamic, while still subtly following it.

- Understand discretion with regard to the personal details of your master, yourself, friends, and associates.
- Be a good and nonjudgmental listener, even for emotionally charged topics.
- Listen without expressing your opinion, on request.
- Be comfortable with giving and receiving nonsexual physical affection (hugs, snuggling, etc.).

Advanced Skills:

- Hosting parties and entertaining large groups.
- Ballroom dancing.
- Detailed knowledge of hobbies and pastimes of interest to your master, and skill in participating in these activities, as appropriate.
- Public entertainment skills – singing, instrumental music, comedy routines, etc.
- Psychological skills for handling difficult people.
- Be charismatic enough in public to lead small groups of people.
- Proficiency in the primary language of anyone who you interact with on a regular basis.
- Maintain a consistently cheerful demeanor in the face of difficult circumstances.

Personal Grooming and Body Service

Remedial Skills:

  Keep yourself clean and reasonably well groomed.

  Dress yourself in a reasonably attractive manner, appropriate for your role and the situation.

  Brush someone else's hair without hurting them.

  Run a bath without fancy soaps/oils.

  Wash someone else's body without injuring them.

  Dry someone else's body without injuring them.

  Lay out an outfit for someone of the same gender, from their clothing supply.

  If appropriate for your role, apply makeup to yourself in a reasonably attractive manner.

Basic Skills:

  Run a bath using fancy soaps/oils.

  Give manicures and pedicures.

  Wash someone else's body in a way that feels luxurious.

  Wash and blow-dry someone else's hair.

  Lay out towels and bath products in a professional-looking manner.

  Shave someone using an electric or safety razor.

  Select and lay out an outfit for someone of any gender, from their clothing supply.

  Apply simple makeup to another person in a reasonably attractive manner.

  Do a simple cleaning and buffing of someone's shoes or boots.

Advanced Skills:

  Create a bath using special teas or spa formulations.

- Make your own luxury bath products.
- Hairdressing (cutting and styling).
- Barbering (including beard grooming and styling).
- Shave someone using an old-fashioned straight razor.
- Do salon-style nails.
- Aesthetician services (buffing, waxing, plucking, etc.)
- Give good wardrobe advice to all genders and do clothing makeovers.
- Professional/theatrical makeup application and makeovers.
- Bootblacking.

Etiquette and Protocol

Remedial Skills:

ॐ Behave reasonably politely and courteously when in public and when with your master.

ॐ Stand and sit with good posture when prompted and when in formal situations.

ॐ Speak clearly without excessive slang or obscenity.

Basic Skills:

ॐ Address specified individuals as "sir" or "ma'am" whenever speaking to them.

ॐ Refrain from using honorifics for people who have asked you not to do so.

ॐ Sit or stand in a specified position, without fidgeting.

ॐ Kneel down and get up from the floor reasonably gracefully, if within your physical capabilities.

ॐ Sit or kneel on the floor for half an hour.

ॐ Speak only when necessary, and in the fewest words that is practical.

ॐ Be aware of scene protocol in your local public group, if applicable, and adhere to it when instructed to do so.

ॐ Bring mistakes to your master's attention in public in a respectful way that does not make them look bad.

ॐ Follow and enforce your master's rules regarding your own behavior or conduct with

> If you have good knees and reasonable balance, try kneeling straight down onto both knees, rather than putting one knee down at a time. To return to standing, come straight up without leaning forward. With a little practice it can be done very smoothly, even while holding something or keeping your hands behind your back. It is one of those silly little things that many masters find charming.

others in a way that does not needlessly draw attention or make others uncomfortable.

❧ Maintain a public demeanor that encourages others to see you as a happy, emotionally well-adjusted person who enjoys helping people. Avoid any behavior that encourages others to assume you are acting against your will, or that your master is unreasonable or abusive.

Advanced Skills:

❧ Understand the scene protocol of a number of BDSM subcultures.

❧ Be comfortable with mainstream formal etiquette.

❧ Organize and serve at a formal dinner.

❧ Gracefully and smoothly speak in passive voice or third person in a way that seems natural and is not jarring or discomfiting to most people.

Sexual Skills

Remedial Skills:

> "Preferred gender" means the gender of the master that the servant is currently in service to, is primarily interested in providing service to, or has the most experience with. Obviously, this distinction is not relevant to all servants.

&. Have experience giving and receiving manual stimulation, oral sex, and some type of penetrative sex.

&. Reach orgasm by some reasonable method in under twenty minutes.

&. Engage in or fantasize about the activities that arouse you without being overwhelmed by guilt or shame.

&. Be reasonably comfortable with your own body, including being fully nude in front of your lover in good lighting.

&. Interact comfortably with the bodies of people you are sexually attracted to, including their genitals and sexual fluids.

&. Understand the basics of birth control (regardless of your sexual orientation) and the prevention of sexually transmitted diseases.

&. If you have a history of abuse or sexual trauma, be able to discuss it in general terms with someone you trust.

Basic Skills:

&. Be experience giving and receiving common sexual activities with your preferred gender. (Oral stimulation, manual stimulation, anal penetration, vaginal penetration, and the use of dildoes, buttplugs, and vibrators.)

&. If you are bisexual, have some sexual experience with both genders. If not, be open-minded about the possibility of providing limited sexual service to your non-preferred gender.

- Be familiar with common SM and fetish activities (spanking, flogging, rope bondage, etc.)
- Be skilled at providing sexual service that is not focused on your own pleasure.
- Be skilled at receiving sexual pleasure, and able to respond with enthusiasm to most common sexual activities, and a variety of SM/fetish activities.
- Be comfortable with the possibility of providing sexual services that seem "dominant" to you.
- Be able to tolerate uncomfortable or moderately painful SM activities that you don't enjoy, without psychological harm.
- Be able to accurately assess whether an activity is putting you at risk for serious physical harm.
- If you have a history of abuse or sexual trauma, be able to discuss it in detail with someone you trust, and understand how it effects your sexual/romantic relationships, your involvement in SM/fetish activities, and your attitude about people having power over others.
- Be very comfortable with your own body, including being looked at by strangers (in a safe environment) when nude or dressed provocatively.
- Be very comfortable interacting sexually with strangers in your preferred age range and gender presentation (in a safe environment) and reasonably comfortable interacting with the adults outside of that range.
- Be able to dress and groom yourself in a sexually appealing manner.

Advanced Skills:

- Be skilled at topping in common SM and fetish activities.
- Be able to eroticize and respond enthusiastically to almost any sexual, fetish, or SM activity that is not excessively painful.

- Be able to tolerate substantially painful SM activities without psychological harm.

- Be able to accurately assess whether an activity is putting you at risk for serious psychological harm.

- Be very comfortable interacting sexually with nearly any adult under reasonably safe circumstances, regardless of weight, age, gender, menstruation, disability, race, or any other personal characteristic.

Books, TV, and Movies About Good Service

Lives of servants on historic British estates:

- Downton Abbey (TV miniseries)
- Upstairs, Downstairs (TV series)
- The Duchess of Duke Street (TV series)
- The Jeeves and Bertie Wooster book series and TV series - *a classic portrayal, even though Joshua objects to Jeeves' attitude.*
- Remains of the Day (book and movie)
- Gosford Park (movie)

Other historic and fantasy media:

- Rome (HBO series) - *with good portrayals of several strong, competent body-servants of famous main characters such as Caesar, Cleopatra, etc.*
- Spartacus: Blood and Sand (TV series) - *with many examples of period servants throughout the show.*
- Lord of the Rings (books and movies) - *especially the relationship between Frodo and Sam.*
- The Batman movies - *look for Alfred, the Batman's batman.*
- The Sherlock Holmes books and movies - *while Watson isn't exactly a servant, he does exemplify the role of the service-oriented sidekick who serves Holmes out of admiration for his brilliance.*
- Family Affair (TV series) - *for Mr. French*
- Diary of a Chambermaid (book and movies)
- The Addams Family (TV series and movies) - *for Lurch and Thing*
- The Miles Vorkosigan book series

About the Authors

Raven Kaldera is a queer FTM transgendered intersexual shaman. He is the author of too many books to list here, including *Dark Moon Rising: Pagan BDSM And The Ordeal Path* and *Power Circuits: Polyamory In A Power Dynamic*. He and his slaveboy Joshua have been teaching and presenting workshops regularly for many years to the BDSM, Neo-Pagan, Sex/Spirituality, transgender, and other communities. 'Tis an ill wind that blows no minds.

Joshua Tenpenny is Raven's Boy, and his devoted assistant, partner, and slave for life. He is a massage therapist, Shiatsu practitioner, and yoga teacher. He is polymorphously perverse, and finds spiritual fulfillment through any kind of worthy service. This is the second book he has co-authored with his master, the first being *Dear Raven And Joshua: Questions And Answers About Master/Slave Relationships*.

Made in United States
Troutdale, OR
03/01/2024